GW00367732

THE BRIDGESTONE
100 BEST PLACES TO STAY IN IRELAND 2006

THE BRIDGESTONE

100 BEST
PLACES TO STAY
IN IRELAND 2006

JOHN McKENNA - SALLY McKENNA

ESTRAGON PRESS

FIRST PUBLISHED IN 2005

BY ESTRAGON PRESS

DURRUS

COUNTY CORK

© ESTRAGON PRESS

TEXT © JOHN & SALLY McKENNA

THE MORAL RIGHT OF THE AUTHORS HAS

BEEN ASSERTED

ISBN 1 874076 71 5

PRINTED IN SPAIN BY GRAPHYCEMS

WRITTEN BY JOHN McKENNA

CONTRIBUTING EDITORS:

EAMON BARRETT

ORLA BRODERICK

ELIZABETH FIELD

CLAIRE GOODWILLIE

LESLIE WILLIAMS

CAROLINE WORKMAN

PUBLISHING EDITOR: SALLY McKENNA

EDITOR: JUDITH CASEY

NI CONTRIBUTER: HARRY OWENS

ART DIRECTION BY NICK CANN

COVER PHOTOS BY MIKE O'TOOLE

ILLUSTRATIONS BY AOIFE WASSER

WEB: FLUIDEDGE.IE

FOR:

Ken and Cathleen Buggy

WITH THANKS TO
Des Collins, Colm Conyngham, Pat Curran,
Julie Barrett, Josette Cadoret, Nick Cann, Frieda Forde,
George Lane, Frank McKevitt, Mike O'Toole,
Miguel Sancho, Hugh Stancliffe,
Ann Marie Tobin, Lorraine Ward.

We greatly appreciate receiving reports, e-mails and
criticisms from readers, and would like to thank those
who have written in the past, whose opinions are of
enormous assistance to us when considering which 100
places to stay finally make it into this book.

Bridgestone is the world's largest tyre and rubber company

• Founded in Japan in 1931, it currently employs over 100,000 people in Europe, Asia and America and its products are sold in more than 150 countries. Its European plants are situated in France, Spain, Italy, Poland and Turkey.

• Bridgestone manufacture tyres for a wide variety of vehicles from passenger cars and motorcycles, trucks and buses to giant earthmovers and aircraft.

• Many new cars are fitted with Bridgestone tyres during manufacture, including Ford, Toyota, Volkswagen, Mercedes and BMW. Ferrari and Porsche are also fitted with Bridgestone performance tyres as original equipment.

• Bridgestone commercial vehicle tyres enjoy a worldwide reputation for durability and its aircraft tyres are used by more than 100 airlines.

• In Formula 1 Bridgestone supply tyres to leading teams and drivers, including Ferrari and Michael Schumacher. Technology developed in the sport has led to increased performance and safety in Bridgestone's road tyres.

• Bridgestone tyres are distributed in Ireland by Bridgestone Ireland Ltd, a subsidiary of the multinational Bridgestone Corporation. A wide range of tyres is stocked in its 70,000 square foot central warehouse and its staff provide sales, technical and delivery services all over Ireland.

• Bridgestone tyres are available from First Stop Tyre Centres and tyre dealers throughout Ireland.

FOR FURTHER INFORMATION:

BRIDGESTONE IRELAND LTD
10 Fingal Bay Business Park
Balbriggan
County Dublin

Tel: + 353 1 841 0000
Fax: + 353 1 841 5245

websites:
www.bridgestone-eu.com
www.firststop-eu.com

• There has never been a time of greater need for a reliable, independent guidebook to places to stay in Ireland. For suddenly, it seems, the country is awash with the financial diaspora of the Celtic Tiger. 4-star joints that sit high on the top of a hill, without a tree in sight, have mushroomed under the blessing of millions of euro spent without a thought to good taste or subtlety.

• Lavishly tarmacadammed up to the door, with a brightly lit fountain that doesn't work, inappropriate decking beside the heli-pad, and PVC windows, the 4-star joint has tassels on every curtain and cushion. It has more marble in the bathroom than Michelangelo ever chiselled. The menu is a facsimile of food. Andrea Bocelli whines on the stereo. The staff pester your kids to order more soft drinks. When the bill arrives, you lose the power of speech and the will to live.

• Irish tourism is under threat, but the threat comes from bad-taste destinations, dodgy tourism developments that litter the coasts, and places that deliver facsimile experiences at fearsome prices. The next time you hear folk from the West complaining that they have no tourists, suggest they go and look out the window at the latest tourism "development". A plague on their houses.

• There are no 4-star joints in this book. instead, there are 100 addresses that show the unique Irish hospitality alive and well, creative, colourful, and blessedly real.

John & Sally McKenna
Durrus, West Cork, October 2005.

"TASTE CLASSIFIES, AND IT CLASSIFIES ITS CLASSIFIER."

PIERRE BOURDIEU

• The question of taste, the question of aesthetic choice, has become the most delicious new skirmishing ground in contemporary Ireland. We are living, after all, in an age when design writers feel confident to say, in weekend newspapers, that to have a set of matching crockery is "vulgar", whilst others will assert, in their defence of some high-falutin' restaurant, that enjoying the experience "is about taste: if you don't have any, you won't enjoy it".

• What an extraordinary thing to say. Surely we all have taste, or tastes, in one way or another? And heaven be with the days when writers on restaurants confined themselves to the question of what tastes were on the plate, before they strode so confidently into the world of aesthetics, paying scant heed on their journey to the French sociologist Pierre Bourdieu's book, *Distinction: A Social Critique of the Judgement of Taste*.

• Well, we had better admit to the "vulgarity" of having a few sets of matching crockery, before asking how taste and aesthetic choice influences who gets into the Bridgestone 100 Best Places to Stay in Ireland. How does our choice of 100 places classify us?

**on top of
their game**

new!

a classic

• Well, what we like is when people set out to design a house, an hotel, a B&B, a restaurant with rooms, in a way that tells you about themselves, their experiences, their choices. A critic should act, in our opinion, merely as a cipher, drawing attention to what is well done, well achieved, well executed, whilst at the same time keeping mum on what sort of design, what sort of aesthetic, they like themselves. Who cares what critics like?

• There are places in this book, then, that may delight your taste, and others that may mystify it: how did they choose this!? Our primary purpose, we believe, is to respect the choices others make, and to avoid those who do things in a clichéd way. Anyone can spend a fortune on design, and effectively waste their money because the finished product tells you nothing about them. This is important, we think, because hospitality is, finally, all about your host.

on top of their game

Aberdeen Lodge, Dublin

Ballymaloe House, Shanagarry

Ballyvolane House, Fermoy

Coast Townhouse, Tramore

Dolphin Beach, Clifden

Fortview House, Goleen

Kelly's Resort Hotel, Rosslare

Killarney Park Hotel, Killarney

Longueville House, Mallow

Merrion Hall, Dublin

The Mill, Dunfanaghy

The Mustard Seed, Echo Lodge, Ballingarry

Newport House, Newport

The Quay House, Clifden

Richmond House, Cappoquin

Salville House, Enniscorthy

Sheen Falls Lodge, Kenmare

Shelburne Lodge, Kenmare

a classic

Anna's House, Comber

Ballynahinch Castle, Recess

Ballyknocken House, Ashford

Blindgate House, Kinsale

Brook Lodge Inn, Macreddin

Carrig House, Killorglin

Coxtown Manor, Donegal

Ghan House, Carlingford

The Glen, Kilbrittain

Glenally House, Youghal

Iskeroon, Caherdaniel

Kilgraney Country House, Bagenalstown

Marble Hall, Dublin

Marlagh Lodge, Ballymena

Sea Mist, Clifden

Temple House, Ballymote

Wineport Lodge, Glasson

new entries and re-entries for 2005

Ballinkeele House, Eniscorthy

Ballymote House, Downpatrick

Bewleys Ballysbridge, Dublin

Cucina, Kinsale

Ferndale, Enniskillen

Grafton House, Dublin

The Green Gate, Ardara

Grove House, Schull

The Inn at Castledawson

Knockeven House, Cobh

Mossie's, Adrigole

The Old Ground, Ennis

Paradiso Rooms, Cork

Paul Arthurs, Kircubbin

Rathmullan House, Rathmullan

Tannery Townhouse, Dungarvan

Vaughan Lodge, Lahinch

• The Bridgestone 100 Best Places to Stay in Ireland is arranged **ALPHABETICALLY, BY COUNTY** so it begins with County Cavan, which is followed by County Clare, and so on. Within the counties, the entries are once again listed alphabetically. Entries in Northern Ireland are itemised alphabetically, at the end of the book. All NI prices are quoted in sterling.

• The contents of the Bridgestone 100 Best Guides are exclusively the result of the authors' deliberations. All meals and accommodation were paid for and any offers of discounts or gifts were refused.

• Many of the places featured in this book are only open during the summer season, which means that they can be closed for any given length of time between October and March.

• **PRICES:** Average prices are calculated on the basis of one night's stay for bed and breakfast.

• **LISTINGS:** In every entry in the book we try to list telephone number, (℡) fax, (🖳). We also list internet details (🖰), where possible, and alert you if you can contact the restaurant by email, or through a specialist web booking service. Most places offer this service, though a few prefer to hear a human voice. We also request details of disabled access(♿), the ability to cater for children, plus any other relevant details.

• **WEBSITES:** Where an entry has a website, we always print the address, as this is the place where you will find most up-to-date information as wel as special offers. All the entries in all the Bridgestone Guides can be found on www.bridgestoneguides.com. See Bridgestone community.

• **BRIDGESTONE PLAQUES:** Look out for our Bridgestone Plaques, displayed by many of our listed establishments.

CONTENTS

BARROWVILLE TOWNHOUSE

Randal & Marie Dempsey
Kilkenny Road
Carlow, County Carlow
© **059-914 3324**
🖷 **059-914 1953**
🖱 **www.barrowvillehouse.com**

Randal and Marie Dempsey's Barrowville could write the book on how to run a townhouse B&B: lots of care, lots of TLC, lots of hard work.

We have remarked often on the fact that it is sheer hard work and application that keeps Randal and Marie Dempsey's smart Carlow townhouse ahead of the pack. Hidden behind a tall wall on the Kilkenny Road just on the outskirts of town, this languorous Victorian house is spacious and cosy and not at all imposing, with comfortable bedrooms that are continually upgraded and improved. But the hard work is most evident in the breakfasts: "We cook our own breads, scones, croissants, jams, marmalades, and breakfast is only cooked to order", says Randal. The buffet table veritably groans under the weight of raspberries, blackberries, blueberries, strawberries, fruit salad, grapefruit, figs, apricots and a fine cheeseboard, and silver pots and bread trays sparkle. When they are ripe, you can even reach overhead and pluck a grape from the vine. "Still more to learn and implement!", says Randal. It seems to us Barrowville could write the book.

- **OPEN:** All year
- **ROOMS:** Seven rooms, all en suite
- **PRICE:** B&B €45-€49.50 per person, €55-€65 single

- **NOTES:** 🖭Visa, Master, Amex. No dinner. No ♿ access. Private car parking. Children over 12 years welcome. 🖱 Email bookings. Computer available for guests to check and send emails.

- **DIRECTIONS:** On the right-hand side after the traffic lights heading south out of Carlow. 80km from Dublin (Route N9); 80km from Rosslare (again N9).

KILGRANEY COUNTRY HOUSE

Bryan Leech & Martin Marley
Bagenalstown
County Carlow
✆ **059-977 5283**
🖷 **059-977 5595**
🖰 **www.kilgraneyhouse.com**

Kilgraney defines the zeitgeist of contemporary
style, interior design, and
modern Irish cooking.

The greatest practitioners of hospitality refract the zeitgeist to their own métier, filtering ideas, moulding con-
cepts, forging everything into their own signature.
If that sounds like abstract psychobabble, then can we
suggest a simple action that will also be supremely pleas-
urable, and which will explain better just what we mean.
Take a trip down to Kilgraney Country House, and just
see how over the last decade Bryan Leech and Martin
Marley have developed, progressed, advanced and
improved this fine old Victorian house, making it into one
of the key destinations in modern Ireland. Kilgraney is
both traditional – the solid hulk of the house – and contemporary – the eclectic style and furnishings. It is guest
house, and sublime self-catering, and this year there is the
new Aroma Spa, a "bespoke aromatherapy centre". Above
all, Kilgraney is utterly individual, with everything forged
into the style signature of these two creative guys.

● **OPEN:** Mar-Nov weekends, Jul-Aug weekly
● **ROOMS:** Six double, en suite rooms
● **PRICE:** B&B €65-€120 per person sharing. Weekend
packages available. Self-catering from €350 per week.

● **NOTES:** 💳Visa, Master, Amex, Laser. Dinner 8pm
€48, communal table (separate dining on request), book
by noon. Wheelchair access with assistance.
Aroma Spa. Children over 12 only.
🖰 Email bookings.

● **DIRECTIONS:**
Just off the R705, 5.5km from Bagenalstown.

MacNEAN TOWNHOUSE

The Maguire family
Blacklion
County Cavan
℡ **071-985 3022**
🖷 **071-985 3404**
🖱 **www.macneanrestaurant.com**

Everyone who travels to Blacklion has great food on their minds, as they arrive at Neven Maguire's brilliant restaurant with its simple rooms.

The plain, three-storey townhouse that is home to Neven Maguire's MacNean restaurant in the tiny hamlet of Blacklion is first choice place to lay your head for the many people who travel from all over the country to eat at this modest temple of contemporary Irish gastronomy. Of course, with only five simple rooms it's not possible for everyone to stay here, and many folk are happy to stay in nearby B&B's. But the situation has galvanised Mr Maguire to develop the number and the specification of the rooms in the townhouse, a promising plan which will make the cooking of one of Ireland's greatest chefs available to even more food lovers.

If the cooking is a glory, so too is the county, yet County Cavan remains overlooked by many visitors who travel up and down the coasts but don't head inland. It is their loss; there are undiscovered glories all around here, and peace and quiet. And finally, a word about breakfast: ace.

● **OPEN:** All year, except Christmas
● **ROOMS:** Four rooms
● **PRICE:** B&B €40 per person sharing, single €45

● **NOTES:** 🖃 Visa, Mastercard.
The MacNean Restaurant opens for Dinner, €55-60.
♿ access.
Children welcome.
Recommended for vegetarians.

● **DIRECTIONS:**
On the main street in Blacklion, which itself is just on the border with Northern Ireland.

THE OLDE POST INN

Tara McCann & Gearoid Lynch
Cloverhill, Butler's Bridge
County Cavan
℡ **047-55555**
🖷 **047-55111**
🖰 **www.theoldepostinn.com**

Mr Lynch and Ms McCann are confidently putting their pretty restaurant with rooms on both the culinary and comfort maps of many people.

Last time we called the Olde Post Inn to see if we could book a room and dinner, we had no luck on either score; full-up, booked-up, very sorry, hope to see you again, thank you for enquiring. It was proof that Mr Lynch's cooking and Ms McCann's hospitality are making waves far beyond the borders of little Butlers Bridge, and proof that cutting-edge operation such as this, with an ace offer of great cooking and fine rooms, have endless potential for success in contemporary Ireland. When people talk about regenerating the BMW region – Border, Midlands, West – what they should be looking at first is the capacity of addresses such as the OPI, or its near-neighbour, The MacNean Townhouse, or Carlingford's Ghan House, to bring in tourists and travellers, thanks to great cooking and great hospitality. At the OPI, Mr Lynch's cooking is the star, beautifully wrought modern Irish food that showcases a stunning technique and beautiful flavours.

- **OPEN:** all year, except Christmas
- **ROOMS:** Seven rooms
- **PRICE:** B&B €40 per person

- **NOTES:** All major cards accepted.
♿ access. Children welcome.
Dinner 6.30pm-9.30pm Tue-Sat; 12.30pm-3pm, 6.30pm-8.30pm Sun, €48.
🖰 Email bookings.

- **DIRECTIONS:**
From Cavan follow N3. At Butler's bridge, take the N54 and the Olde Post is 3km further, on the right.

MOY HOUSE

Antoin O'Looney
Lahinch
County Clare
℡ 065-708 2800
🖳 065-708 2500
🖱 www.moyhouse.com

Moy House offers some of the most amazing sea views of any Irish country house, whilst Bernie Merry makes sure everything else is just tip-top.

They don't build houses like Moy House any more, gothic-baroque indulgences from the century before last, complete with a central tower for ascending and then surveying the celestial light as it dies over Lahinch Bay. It's a preposterous place, and it's mighty fun, thanks to that very preposterousness: staying here feels like being in some children's story, as the scale of the house dwarfs you, and you feel part of some ace adventure.

But, unlike other gothic-baroque piles in Ireland, Moy has been beautifully and sensitively restored, and it works like clockwork, thanks to Bernie Merry and her crew, who are super-capable. Everything about the house feels like an indulgence, especially the epic baths and their array of unguents, the extraordinary views over the bay, and the splendour and whacky unorthodoxy of the public rooms. Cooking is conservative and capable and thereby suits the out-of-time nature of the place. Superbly surreal.

- ● **OPEN:** Mid Jan-end Dec
- ● **ROOMS:** Nine rooms
- ● **PRICE:** €200-€239 double room, €127-€159 single.

- ● **NOTES:** 💳All major cards accepted.
Special offers Nov-May. Group rates accepted.
Dinner for residents, €45.
🖱 Email bookings.

- ● **DIRECTIONS:**
Moy House is located about 1.5km south of Lahinch town, on the Miltown Malbay road. Shannon Airport is 1 hour's drive.

THE OLD GROUND HOTEL

Allen Flynn
O'Connell Street
Ennis, County Clare
© **065-682 8127**
🖱 **www.oldgroundhotel.com**

Kindly ladies who call you "pet", stylish rooms, nice food in the bistro, that's the Old Ground potion.

We reckoned they had all gone to that great hotel in the sky, those kindly ladies, of advancing years, who march around the hotel breakfast room, taking your order, bringing your tea, and who call you 'pet' or 'love' or maybe even 'dear'. Well, if that is your idea of who you want to look after you first thing in the morning, then stay at the spick and span Old Ground Hotel. For there, amidst many other kindly staff who seem to be getting a great buzz from their work, you will meet the Breakfast Room lady who calls you 'pet', or 'love', or 'dear'.

Mind you, there are other reasons to choose the Old Ground. Ever since they created the new 4th and 5th floors last year, they have shown just how to do a hotel room that is classy, comfortable and splendidly commodious without being at all over-the-top: these are some of the best rooms we have stayed in in Ireland recently, and the cooking in their bistro, the Town Hall, is very good.

● **OPEN:** Mid Jan-end Dec
● **ROOMS:** Nine rooms
● **PRICE:** €110-€200 double room, €85-115 single.

● **NOTES:** 📷All major cards accepted. ♿ access. The adjacent Townhall Bistro, owned by the hotel, is a Bridgestone recommended restaurant. 🖱 On-line bookings.

● **DIRECTIONS:**
Smack in the centre of Ennis, on the corner of O'Connell Street and Station Road.

STELLA MARIS

The Haugh family
Kilkee
County Clare
℡ **065-905 6455**
🖷 **065-906 0006**
🖑 **www.stellamarishotel.com**

A small, family-run, seaside hotel, the Haugh family's Stella Maris is all about the old things – personable service, care, comfort – all done well.

Situated right on the street corner's edge, just up the street from the strand in little Kilkee, Ann Haugh's resort hotel is one of those nice, cosy, comfy old-style, family-run coastal hotels that were once a staple of Ireland's hospitality culture, particularly in holiday towns like Kilkee, but which have declined in number so spectacularly in recent years.

Stella Maris has 19 rooms, simple, clean, comfortable spaces that probably won't appeal to style fashionistas, but they do appeal to us, and in particular to a nostalgic yearning for hospitality that once wasn't exclusively caught up with the latest, the newest and the chicest. What counts in Stella Maris is the welcome, the hospitality, the blazing fire in the reception, tea taken looking out on the strand, a nice relaxed dinner of Carrigaholt crab claws, then monkfish wrapped in Parma ham or Kilkee lamb baked in the oven. The simple things, done well.

- **OPEN:** All year
- **ROOMS:** 19 rooms, all en suite
- **PRICE:** €40-€65 per person sharing, single supplement for single occupancy of double room €20-€30

- **NOTES:** 🖬 All major cards accepted.
Children welcome. No ♿ access to bedrooms.
Two bars, one restaurant, dinner main courses €12-€26. Private parking. 🖑 Email bookings.
Pet friendly.

- **DIRECTIONS:**
In the centre of Kilkee, overlooking the bay.

VAUGHAN LODGE

Michael & Maria Vaughan
Vaughan Lodge,
Lahinch, Co Clare
℡ **065-708 1111**
🖷 **065-708 1011**
🖯 **www.vaughanlodge.ie**

Michael and Maria Vaughan's smart new hotel and restaurant is a welcome return for the Vaughans of Lahinch.

Readers with long memories will recall that Mr Eamon's was the Lahinch restaurant staple of the Bridgestone guides all during the 1990's, when Eamon and Rita Vaughan ran an outstanding restaurant, characterised not only by fine cooking, but also by exemplary service.

Well, that exemplary service from the Vaughan family is back, as Michael and Maria Vaughan have quietly opened Vaughan Lodge, a 22-room hotel with a bar and bistro. The style throughout is one of comfortable understatement, which makes for an exceptionally relaxing place to eat and stay, with nice food in the restaurant – comforting dishes like seared scallops or Clare goat's cheese to begin, then cod with crabmeat or lamb wrapped in mint pancakes, and excellent puddings. Above all, you get looked after in Vaughan Lodge, the staff are tuned to your needs with an almost telepathic sympathy, so everything bodes promisingly for the Vaughans of Vaughan Lodge.

● **OPEN:** All year apart from Jan-Feb.
● **ROOMS:** 22 rooms, all en suite
● **PRICE:** €115-€155 per person sharing.
Single €155-€205

● **NOTES:** 🖃All major cards accepted.
♿ access. Restaurant, dinner €40.
Private car parking.
Children welcome. 🖯 Email bookings.

● **DIRECTIONS:**
From Ennis, take the Ennistymon road, cross over the bridge, take Lahinch road, and it's 2.4km on the left.

AHERNE'S

The Fitzgibbon family
163 North Main Street
Youghal, East Cork
✆ **024-92424**
🖷 **024-93633**
🖰 **www.ahernes.com**

The ageless Aherne's of Youghal is truly a classic Inn: restaurant, bars, and accommodation that give you exactly what you need and want.

Aherne's is an Irish inn in the classical tradition. An edge-of-town address with stylish bars, a benchmark restaurant, and rooms; Aherne's is tasteful in every way, from the super-efficient and personable service, led by the family members themselves, to the delicious cooking in the restaurant and bars, to the smart, stylish rooms and suites they have developed over the last decade.

It is one of those long-established addresses that works with a ruthless efficiency and a rigorous self-discipline to keep itself up to the mark, which means that Aherne's never dates, never goes out of fashion, remains always at the cutting edge. It is not just a staple of the Bridgestone Guides, but a staple of the best kind of Irish hospitality. They look after you in Aherne's.

David Fitzgibbon's cooking in the clubby, somewhat masculine dining room is a summation of contemporary and classical fish cookery, cooking with a rich signature style.

- **OPEN:** All year, except Christmas
- **ROOMS:** 12 rooms, all en suite
- **PRICE:** €80-€115 per person sharing, Single from €110

- **NOTES:** 🖭All major cards accepted. Dinner €42. Children welcome, 50% reduction for young children, 33% reduction for third adult.
♿ access. Secure parking. 🖰 Email bookings.

- **DIRECTIONS:**
Aherne's is very well signposted in Youghal, a large yellow building on the right-hand side if travelling east.

ASHLEE LODGE

Anne & John O'Leary
Tower, Blarney
County Cork
℡ **021-438 5346**
🖰 **www.ashleelodge.com**

Anne and John O'Leary over-deliver in every way for their guests in Ashlee Lodge, which makes this a special, supremely comfortable place to stay.

In our efforts to describe Ashlee Lodge last year, when it made its debut in the Bridgestones, we said of Anne and John O'Leary: "In modern marketing parlance, they over-deliver".

Well, you can scrap the marketing parlance, for a better term than the management mumbo-jumbo is, simply, care. Stay in Ashlee, and what you will remember is how the O'Learys have cared for you. A lift into town? No problem. A pick-up from the airport/golf course/train station? No problem. A snack when you arrive? No problem. Information about how best to handle your hormonal teenage children? No problem,

Actually we didn't get around to asking what to do with the teenagers, but we know that if we had asked, that John would have downloaded some stuff whilst Anne would have called a friend in the psychiatric business. Overdelivering, or what? Well, better to just call it care.

● **OPEN:** All year except 22 Dec-7 Jan
● **ROOMS:** 10 rooms, all en suite, made up of 6 executive rooms, 2 mini suites and 2 master suites
● **PRICE:** €70 for executive room, €80 for mini suite, €100 for master suite, per person sharing

● **NOTES:** 🖵All major cards accepted. Dinner Tue-Sat, mains €18-€23 ♿ access. No facilities for children. Secure parking. 🖰 Email bookings. Pet friendly.

● **DIRECTIONS:**
From Blarney, take the R617 for 1.5km journey to Tower.

BALLYMALOE HOUSE

The Allen family
Shanagarry
Midleton, East Cork
✆ **021-465 2531**
🖷 **021-465 2021**
🖰 **www.ballymaloe.com**

No matter how often you stay at Ballymaloe House, every visit always feels special, exciting, delightful.

" This is the heart of the Irish food culture, everything that is best stems from the evangelical approach taken here, it can be no purer than Ballymaloe - it is the heart, and it is beating fantastically well."

Our editor Eamon Barrett chooses his words carefully, and how significant that he should have used the term "evangelical" when talking about his first visit to Ballymaloe House, the Allen family's legendary east Cork country house, and the address that has inspired so many imitators, and inspired so many breathless memories of staying at this great address. And what are the Allen family crusading on behalf of? World-class hospitality, world-class cooking, world-class care, no more than that. Over the last year we have been to a wedding here, to two working dinners, and to a spot of r'n'r, and every occasion was nothing less than special, every visit felt unique, a chance to explore and understand the mother lode.

● **OPEN:** All year
● **ROOMS:** 34 rooms. No suites
● **PRICE:** B&B €100-€150 per person sharing. Single €120-€175. Spare bed €45

● **NOTES:** 🖻All major cards accepted. Dinner 7pm-9.30pm, €62. Recommended for vegetarians. Children welcome, cot, high chair, early dinner. Private parking. 🖰 On-line bookings.

● **DIRECTIONS:**
From Cork take N25 to exit for Whitegate R630, follow signs for R629 Cloyne. House is 3.2km beyond Cloyne.

10 PLACES FOR
GREAT ROMANCE

1

BALLYVOLANE
CASTLELYONS, Co CORK

2

THE BROOK LODGE INN
MACREDDIN, Co WICKLOW

3

COAST TOWNHOUSE
TRAMORE, Co WATERFORD

4

THE GLEN
KILBRITTAIN, Co CORK

5

ISKEROON
CAHERDANIEL, Co KERRY

6

KNOCKEVEN
COBH, Co CORK

7

THE MUSTARD SEED
BALLINGARRY, Co LIMERICK

8

STELLA MARIS
BALLYCASTLE, Co MAYO

9

TANNERY TOWNHOUSE
DUNGARVAN, Co WATERFORD

10

ZUNI
KILKENNY, Co KILKENNY

BALLYMAKEIGH HOUSE

Margaret Browne
Killeagh
East Cork
℡ **024-95184**
🖷 **024-95370**
🖰 **www.ballymakeighhouse.com**

Excellent country cooking, good country comfort and a warm welcome from Margaret make Ballymakeigh a very difficult place to bid farewell.

You can tell how ambitious a cook Margaret Browne is not simply by looking at her dinner and breakfast menus, mouth-watering though they may be, but instead by looking at the excellent wine list she has compiled. In many B&B's the list is a token offering, with bottles that will get you wet inside but not do a whole lot more. But in Ballymakeigh the list is better than many restaurants and hotels. So, check in, order up a bottle of Martin Codax Albarino to start, and settle in for dinner and enjoy the serious cooking of a woman who is one of few B&B keepers to actually have written a recipe book of her cooking.

Next morning, promising yourself the diet starts tomorrow, start with fresh juices, and porridge with whiskey, and then The Final Fling: The Full Irish? Boiled egg with toast soldiers? Scottish kippers? Home-made marmalade on hot toast? Scrambled eggs? The diet starts tomorrow.

● **OPEN:** Valentine weekend-1 Nov
● **ROOMS:** Six rooms, all en suite
● **PRICE:** B&B €55-€60 per person, single supplement charged high season only, €10

● **NOTES:** Amex, Visa, Mastercard. Dinner 7.30pm-8.30pm, €40-€45. No wheelchair access.
Enclosed car park. Children welcome, babysitting, 50% reduction for children when sharing.
🖰 Email bookings.

● **DIRECTIONS:**
Signposted on the N25, 9.5km west of Youghal.

BALLYVOLANE

Justin & Jenny Green
Castlelyons
Fermoy, North Cork
✆ **025-36349**
🖨 **025-36781**
🖰 **www.ballyvolanehouse.ie**

"So this is what it is like to live like a lord!" wrote Howard Jacobson about the brilliant Ballyvolane.

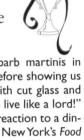

"Justin and Jenny Green serve us rhubarb martinis in front of a log fire in the drawing room before showing us the way to a communal table flashing with cut glass and polished silver. So this is what it is like to live like a lord!" That was the writer Howard Jacobson's reaction to a dinner at Ballyvolane, which he described in New York's *Food & Wine* Magazine. Mr Jacobson praised the "decadent" jerusalem artichoke soup, and the turbot with salsa verde, and, with typical acuity, noted that the Ballyvolane experience is "conceived and put together with a boldness that can only come from someone who has knocked around the world a bit". Indeed, the Greens have blue-chip global experience behind them, and they have used it to animate Ballyvolane to the heights. This is one of the great country houses, and it offers one of the greatest country house experiences. And, best of all, Justin and Jenny have only started – there are exciting plans afoot.

● **OPEN:** 1 Jan-23 Dec
● **ROOMS:** Six rooms, all en suite
● **PRICE:** B&B €75-€95 per person sharing. €30 single supplement.

● **NOTES:** 📷 Visa, Access, Amex. Dinner 8pm, €47.50, communal table. ♿ access. Private car park. Children welcome. Self catering also available. Pet friendly. 🖰 Email bookings.

● **DIRECTIONS:**
From the N8, south just after Rathcormac, take the turn to Midleton and look for the sign for the house.

BLINDGATE HOUSE

Maeve Coakley
Blindgate, Kinsale
West Cork
✆ **021-477 7858**
🖨 **021-477 7868**
🖰 **www.blindgatehouse.com**

One of the most sensual
and inspiring houses,
Blindgate has perfect feng
shui: just feel that luxury.

Maeve Coakley's Blindgate House is one of those places that makes you feel fantastic.

The feng shui of the public rooms and the bedrooms in this modern house just up the hill from the centre of Kinsale is so pitch perfect that it achieves a positively sensual effect. This is a most tactile house, an address where fabrics, furnishings, art works and hospitality all commingle to give the customer what feels like nothing less than an arresting big hug of comfort. The design of this dream destination is so acutely achieved that it lifts your spirits just to walk in the door. You can only achieve this sort of effect by being fiercely ambitious, and the determination to achieve stellar standards is equally evident in Ms Coakley's cooking at breakfast. Once again, this cooking has a luxurious sensuality to it, thanks to freshness, judgement, good ingredients, above all thanks to simple good taste. Blindgate House makes you feel like a million dollars.

● **OPEN:** Mar-Dec
● **ROOMS:** 11 rooms (seven twin rooms, three standard double rooms & one superior double)
● **PRICE:** B&B €115-€170 per room

● **NOTES:** 🖼Visa, Mastercard, Amex. No dinner. ♿ access with assistance, but no walk-in showers. Ample enclosed parking. No children under 8 years. 🖰 Email bookings.

● **DIRECTIONS:**
200m past St Multose Church – just up the hill from the Kinsale Gourmet Store.

BOW HALL

Dick & Barbara Vickery
Castletownshend
West Cork
✆ **028-36114**
✆ **dvicbowhall@eircom.net**

Barbara and Dick Vickery's beautiful Bow Hall is a truly special place, animated by the ageless energy of this effervescent, unstoppable woman.

"We've been doing this for 27 years!" exclaims Barbara Vickery, "We just don't know how to stop!"
Now that may not sound too remarkable a thing for Mrs Vickery to say about her work and that of her husband, Dick, in their lovely B&B in lovely Castletownshend. But consider this: Mrs Vickery started Bow Hall at an age when everyone else is retiring. She has seen four score years and more. And she leps around the place like a kid, unstoppable.
Bow Hall is exactly the sort of house you dream of finding in a charming, idiosyncratic, surreal little village like Castletownshend. It is relaxed, relaxing, its three rooms consummately stylish in an ageless way, with American design influences mutated through a West Cork sensibility. And ageless is just the right word, come to think of it. Mrs Vickery and her house have an ageless energy and brio that is the soul of hospitality itself. 27 more, we say.

● **OPEN:** All year, except Christmas
● **ROOMS:** Three rooms, all with private baths
● **PRICE:** €50 per person sharing,
Single supplement €5

● **NOTES:** 🖳No credit cards accepted.
Dinner 8pm, communal table, by reservation only, €35.
No & access. Enclosed car park.
Children welcome.

● **DIRECTIONS:**
On the right-hand side of the road when heading down the steep hill.

PARADISO ROOMS

Denis Cotter & Bridget Healy
16 Lancaster Quay
Cork, County Cork
✆ **021-427 7939**
🖷 **021-427 4973**
🖑 **www.cafeparadiso.ie**

The brand new trio of Paradiso Rooms are as wildly original and colourful as the restaurant's fab cookery.

Denis Cotter and Bridget Healy simply don't do things the way other people do them. The three rooms they have created for visitors to Café Paradiso are unlike any other rooms in Ireland: they are more colourful, more simple, with huge tarpa wallhangings, tiny tiki charms on the walls, with shopping bags used as design objects alongside ace prints by Debbie Godsil.

And, of course, when it comes to breakfast, they have re-invented that too: grilled Portobello mushroom in sage butter with crushed potato cake and sweet and hot pepper jam; scrambled eggs with chives and lovage with roast plum tomatoes and cannellini beans; buttermilk pancakes with caramelised apples, maple syrup and vanilla mascarpone; crumpets with blueberry compote and cream. The rooms and the breakfast and dinner in CP all add up to a typically original and irresistible offer from these outrageously free thinkers. Paradiso Rooms are to die for.

- **OPEN:** All year, except Christmas
- **ROOMS:** Three double rooms, all en suite
- **PRICE:** B&B, €160 per room

- **NOTES:** 💳 Visa, Mastercard. Dinner in the restaurant essential part of the package, €45. Breakfast menu also served in Cafe Paradiso restaurant. No ♿ access.
🖑 Email bookings. Spare bed available for a child.

- **DIRECTIONS:**
The Western Road leads away from Cork city centre to the University area. Cafe Paradiso is opposite the Lancaster Lodge, on your right as you head west.

CUCINA

Ursula Roncken
9 Market Street,
Kinsale,
County Cork
℡ **021-470 0707**
🖰 **www.cucina.ie**

The style of Ursula Roncken's Cucina is deceptively simple, and hides a lot of smart style choices.

Ursula Roncken's Cucina has carved out a reputation as one of the key new arrivals in Kinsale, a town rapidly regaining the culinary reputation it has lost to towns such as Kenmare in recent times. The small, streetside dining room of the restaurant is brilliantly designed, something you appreciate when you see just how relaxed people are in here: at their ease, enjoying the good food and, in particular, enjoying truly great service from a brilliant team of staff who are amongst the best we have seen in the course of the last year – these girls are special. At any time of day, this room feels good.

Upstairs then there are three simple rooms to repair to after a good dinner either downstairs or elsewhere in town. The style of Cucina is deceptively simple, but Ms Roncken has worked hard to get this restaurant with rooms just right and it feels right. One drawback, if you stay Saturday, is that they don't serve breakfast on Sunday.

● **OPEN:** all year, apart from two weeks at Christmas.
● **ROOMS:** 3 double rooms, all en suite
● **PRICE:** €60 per person sharing, room only rate, no breakfast, though café opens early.

● **NOTES:** 🖃No credit cards accepted.
Café open 9am-5pm, Mon-Sat. Breakfast served 9am-11.30pm, Lunch 11.30pm-4pm. 🖰 Email bookings.

● **DIRECTIONS:**
In the centre of Kinsale, opposite the Kinsale Crystal shop.

FORTVIEW HOUSE

Violet Connell
Gurtyowen, Toormore,
Goleen, West Cork
✆ **028-35324**
📠 **028-35324**
🖱 **www.fortviewhousegoleen.com**

Everyone's favourite West
Cork B&B, Violet Connell's
Fortview House is a fantas-
tic style and food temple.

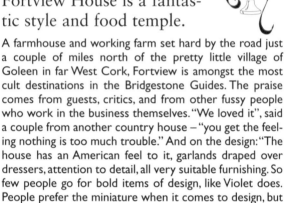

A farmhouse and working farm set hard by the road just
a couple of miles north of the pretty little village of
Goleen in far West Cork, Fortview is amongst the most
cult destinations in the Bridgestone Guides. The praise
comes from guests, critics, and from other fussy people
who work in the business themselves. "We loved it", said
a couple from another country house – "you get the feeling nothing is too much trouble." And on the design: "The
house has an American feel to it, garlands draped over
dressers, attention to detail, all very suitable furnishing. So
few people go for bold items of design, like Violet does.
People prefer the miniature when it comes to design, but
Violet's kitchen had these bold vessels, in a cottage environment - we were fascinated!" And, all agree, at
Fortview you are getting something special for the forty
or so euro that you pay for bed and the legendary, extra-
generous breakfast. Gorgeous and such terrific value.

- **OPEN:** 1 March-1 Nov
- **ROOMS:** Five rooms, all en suite
- **PRICE:** B&B €45 per person sharing

- **NOTES:** 💳All major cards accepted.
Dinner strictly by prior arrangement only, €35.
Two self-catering houses available.
No ♿ access. Enclosed car park.
Children over 6 years welcome.

- **DIRECTIONS:**
Signposted 2km from Toormore on the main Durrus
road (R591). 12km from Durrus, 9km from Goleen.

GARNISH HOUSE

Con & Hansi Lucey
Western Road
Cork City, County Cork
© 021-427 5111
📠 021-427 3872
🖰 www.garnish.ie

Garnish House is garnished with the solicitude of Hansi Lucey, a solicitude no one who stays at this ace Cork B&B can fail to be charmed by.

Our friends Val and Jim had a couple of weeks in Cork in August 2005 and when they got back to the 'States they wrote, "We loved Rock Cottage, Paradiso, and Hansi's B&B, and watching the swimmers in the first River Lee swim in 50 years".

What is interesting about this trio of Bridgestone stars is that Garnish House becomes "Hansi's B&B". And that's what Garnish House is all about: Hansi Lucey. There are droves and scores of B&B's on the Western Road, but only one of them has Hansi at the helm, and that is the USP of Garnish House. Mrs Lucey is the personification of hospitality, right down to enquiring, just as you are on the point of finishing the biggest, bumperest breakfast in Cork, whether or not you might like a chocolate eclair, perhaps? Oh go on! You will! You will!

So, whatever trio of favourites emerge from your own next trip to Cork, "Hansi's B&B" is certain to be there.

● **OPEN:** All year
● **ROOMS:** 14 rooms, all en suite
● **PRICE:** B&B €76-€130 per room, €70-€90 single

● **NOTES:** 💳All major cards accepted. No dinner. Limited ♿ access. Enclosed car parking. Children welcome, high chair, cot, babysitting, reduction if sharing. Self-catering accommodation available.
🖰 Email bookings.

● **DIRECTIONS:**
Five minutes' walk from the city centre, just opposite UCC.

THE GLEN

Diana & Guy Scott
Kilbrittain
West Cork
℡ 023-49862
🖰 www.glencountryhouse.ie

The Glen is a house with the West Cork magic. At the edge of the sea, it feels like the centre of the world.

Approached through an avenue of arching trees, just a stone's throw from the coastal road that runs from Kinsale westwards on to Clonakilty, The Glen is a large Georgian house set in a mature, handsome garden, with a pretty walled garden to the side of the house. It's one of those houses that actually makes you want to own it the second you see it; that's how archetypal it is.

But, if you can't own it, you can happily stay here in its glorious, cultured comfort. Diana Scott is both a fantastic hostess and a fantastic cook who turns an artistic and capable hand to the making of breakfast: fresh raspberries from the garden, light, fluffy pancakes, benchmark scrambled eggs with Ummera salmon. The design of the rooms is country classic, timeless and elegant, comfortable and cossetting, with careful use of a very individual collection of modern Irish paintings. The Glen has that indefinable West Cork Thing, a touch of magic, a touch of brilliance.

- ● **OPEN:** Easter-1 Nov
- ● **ROOMS:** Four rooms and one family unit
- ● **PRICE:** B&B €75 per person sharing, €15 single supplement. €175 for family unit.

- ● **NOTES:** 📼Visa Mastercard accepted.
No dinner. No ♿ access.
Secure car parking. Children welcome.
🖰 Email bookings. Pet friendly.

- ● **DIRECTIONS:**
Signposted from the R600, approximately half way between Clonakilty and Kinsale.

GLENALLY HOUSE

Fred & Herta Rigney
Copperalley, Youghal
East Cork
℡ **024-91623**
🖰 **www.glenally.com**

Rigorous, original, wildly
inventive, Glenally fuses
old styles and new styles
with brilliant panache.

Attention style lovers: if you haven't been to the glorious
Glenalley, then you are missing the chance to be inspired
by one of the great style icon destinations, and by two of
the great style doctors in Fred and Herta.

Everything in Glenally is considered, everything made
memorable by the intellectual use of colour, the arrangement of flowers, even by leaving an item wild, isolated or
untouched. You gasp at the daring of putting six individual
red nasturtium flowers into six jam jars on a mantelpiece,
or the three little boxes of Lux soap on an otherwise
empty bathroom shelf. The sparkly grey floor in the otherwise white bathrooms. The lush jewel-striped red and
green curtains of a bedroom matching an old gilt mirror
that has been painted green and draped with red rose
lighting. This is an extraordinary house, run by two vivid
and meticulous people. If you go there, check the walled
garden which they describe as their *real* passion. Wow!

● **OPEN:** 1 Mar-mid Dec. Reservations only Dec-Feb
● **ROOMS:** Four rooms, 3 all en suite, 1 private bath
● **PRICE:** B&B €45-€65 per person sharing, €15 single
supplement.

● **NOTES:** Visa, Mastercard. Dinner, 8pm, €40. BYO.
No ♿ access. Secure car parking.
No facilities for under 12s. 🖰 Email bookings.

● **DIRECTIONS:**
From roundabout east of Clockgate, continue straight
on N25 past Esso, 250m, take first left. After 75m turn
right and go to end of lane (200m) and through gates.

GROVE HOUSE

Katarina Runske
Colla Road, Schull
West Cork
✆ **028-28067**
🖷 **028-28069**
🖱 **www.grovehouseschull.com**

Katarina Runske and her
mother, Katherine Noren,
are the new force behind
the beautiful Grove House.

In a new incarnation under Katarina Runske, Schull's
beautiful Grove House will reintroduce the legendary
Katherine Noren, Katarina's mother, back into a West
Cork kitchen. This is great news for those who loved Mrs
Noren's cooking in Dunworley Cottage in Butlerstown,
where she produced some of the most original and delicious food in Ireland. "It will be a family place, my son Max
will help me in front of house, and my son Nico is dying
to get back to helping granny in the kitchen", says
Katarina, who herself has many years of hospitality experience, working in various Kinsale restaurants.

The combination of Grove House's beautiful Georgian
rooms and elegant public spaces with a cutting-edge
restaurant is just what Schull needs. "I want everyone to
feel comfortable, at ease and welcome", says Katrina, and
after the distinguished stewardship of this lovely house
under Billy and Mary O'Shea, Grove House is reborn.

● **OPEN:** all year
● **ROOMS:** Five double rooms
● **PRICE:** B&B low season €80, high season €100-
€120 per room, sharing. Single supplement €25

● **NOTES:** Restaurant open 7 days in summer, week-
ends only off season. Dinner always available for guests.
Private parking. 🖱 Email bookings.
Pet friendly.

● **DIRECTIONS:**
Take left opposite AIB, turn onto Colla Road, Grove
House is about 500 metres on the right-hand side.

KNOCKEVEN

John & Pam Mulhaire
Rushbrooke,
Cobh, Co Cork
✆ **021-481 1778**
🖩 **021-481 1719**
🖱 **www.knockevenhouse.com**

Pamela Mulhaire's elegant
house in Cobh enjoys svelte
style, super cooking, and
the patron's great energy.

Pamela Mulhaire has only been running Knockeven as a
guest house for a little over a year, but the level of accom-
plishment and comfort she has succeeded in creating in
that space of time, not to mention her mastery of hospitality, would have you believing she had been at the old
hospitality game all her life.

The rooms are extra-comfortable, and offer serious pampering with good toiletries, fluffy robes, and showers that
could pummel Peter Jackson's King Kong into blissful sub-
mission. The house itself is a sweet oasis of privacy overlooking the harbour in Cobh, but what makes it special is
Mrs Mulhaire's unstoppable personality: she makes you
feel not merely welcome, but extra-welcome, double-
welcome, triple-welcome, and she makes a super breakfast, starting with a great buffet and continuing with ace
scrambled eggs with smoked salmon. Value for money is
super, and all Cobh needs now is a good restaurant.

● **OPEN:** all year, except Christmas
● **ROOMS:** Four double rooms
● **PRICE:** B&B €100-€120 per room, person sharing.
Single €65-75

● **NOTES:** No dinner. No ♿ access. Private parking.
Children welcome. 🖱 Email bookings.

● **DIRECTIONS:**
Leave the N25 Cork Rosslare road onto the R624,
direction Cobh. Pass Fota, cross over the bridge and
take the first right. At Great Island Motors turn left and
it's the first avenue on the left.

LONGUEVILLE HOUSE

The O'Callaghan family
Mallow
North Cork
℡ 022-47156
📠 022-47459
🖱 www.longuevillehouse.ie

There is a primal energy at work in the lovely Longueville, making for one of Ireland's greatest destinations.

A bumper, pink, Palladian mansion high on a hill a few miles west of Mallow, Longueville House is the historic home of the O'Callaghans, and it is one of the supreme destinations to enjoy the magnificence of Irish country life. "There is no other restaurant I can think of where the food produced by the kitchen tastes so much of the land. It is the complete country estate", our editor Eamon Barrett wrote recently, and Mr Barrett was especially knocked out by "the friendly ambience throughout the whole place, led by the charming Aisling O'Callaghan".

As Mrs O'Callaghan is to front-of-house, so William O'Callaghan is to the kitchen, a remarkable cook in full control of his métier, transforming the ruddiest of country ingredients into the most ethereal, subtle, unforgettable dishes. The conservatory gets our vote as the most romantic dining room in the country, lazing in the lounge in the afternoon is our dearest dream, Longueville is ace.

● **OPEN:** Mar-Nov & enquire low season. Open for Christmas.
● **ROOMS:** 20 rooms, all en suite
● **PRICE:** B&B €180-€260 per room. Supplements apply for superior rooms and suites.

● **NOTES:** 📟All major cards accepted. Dinner served from 6.30pm, €55. Recommended for for vegetarians. Children welcome. Small weddings. 🖱 On-line bookings.

● **DIRECTIONS:**
5km west of Mallow on the N72 to Killarney. Look for the large sign.

MOSSIE'S

David & Lorna Ramshaw
Trafrask, Adrigole, Beara
West Cork
℡ **027-60606**
🖰 **www.mossiesrestaurant.com**

The country charms of Ulusker House, home to Mossie's, are expressed in a very singular aesthetic.

Plan to arrive at Mossie's in late afternoon, check into the pretty rooms, take in the view from the verandah, then take some tea in the garden. Now, gird your loins, and drag yourself a few miles up the hill at the back of the house to Ballynahower Wedge Grave. At times you may feel like giving up: don't. The views from the summit are astounding, a light show put on by the elements entirely for your benefit.

And now, what an appetite you have for dinner in Mossie's restaurant, a series of three small rooms downstairs in the blue-hued, country charm of Ulusker House. There are daily specials chalked on the blackboard – lemon sole with shrimp and asparagus, lobster thermidor, summer pudding – and what a great time it is you are having. There is no mystery as to why this should be: David and Lorna Ramshaw have both a rigorous work ethic, and a finely nuanced aesthetic, and they make Mossie's magic.

● **OPEN:** All year apart from three weeks in Jan.
● **ROOMS:** Five rooms, all en suite
● **PRICE:** B&B €70-€140 per room for double occupancy, single occupancy €45-€85
● **CREDIT CARDS:** Visa, Mastercard

● **NOTES:** Restaurant opens for garden lunch (€12), dinner, (€34) & Sun lunch. (€20). ♿ access. Pet friendly. 🖰 Email bookings. Closed Mon & Tue off season.

● **DIRECTIONS:**
12 minutes from Glengarriff, follow the Castletownbere road, and look for signs in Adrigole.

OTTO'S CREATIVE CATERING

Otto & Hilda Kunze
Dunworley, Butlerstown
Bandon, West Cork
© **023-40461**
🖰 **www.ottoscreativecatering.com**

The holistic vision of hospitality embraced by Otto and Hilda at the remote, sea-swept OCC is powerful and profound, and unforgettable.

Certain people have thought so deeply about the concept of hospitality, of the concept of cooking and of the value of hospitality, that the way in which they offer these services becomes completely radical, utterly individual.

Otto and Hilda Kunze are just such a pair of individuals, two radical revolutionaries, people whose entire vision of hospitality and cooking is completely distinctive, completely their own, formed from hard work and deep thinking, an all-encompassing vision.

OCC is not like any other place to stay and eat in Ireland. The vision Otto and Hilda have is completely holistic: you don't go to OCC, you escape to it, you liberate yourself from the normal world to be at this simple but vital spa for the soul in wild, wonderful, sea-swept Dunworley. Combined with the astonishing cooking of Mr Kunze, a chef whose food is sui generis, this retreat for the senses will leave you feeling rejuvenated, indeed feeling re-born.

● **OPEN:** All year
● **ROOMS:** Two double rooms and self-catering cottage
● **PRICE:** B&B €60 per person sharing, €20 single supplement.
● **CREDIT CARDS:** Visa, Mastercard, Laser

● **NOTES:** Dinner served Wed-Sat, €50; Sun lunch €35. No wheelchair access. Secure parking. Children welcome. 🖰 Email bookings. Pet friendly.

● **DIRECTIONS:**
From Bandon go to Timoleague, follow signs to Barryroe until you come across signs to Dunworley.

PIER HOUSE

Ann & Pat Hegarty
Pier Road
Kinsale
West Cork
✆ **021-477 4475**
www.pierhousekinsale.com

Ann Hegarty's funky and stylish Pier House is a great Kinsale home, a place that really fizzles with the energy of rollicking, renewed Kinsale.

Kinsale is getting back into the groove again. Cucina has opened. Fishy Fishy will have two restaurants by early 2006. Toddie's is knocking 'em dead in the old Kinsale Brewery and, right at the heart of this renaissance, is Ann and Pat Hegarty's cracking Pier House, a splendid B&B that matches the standards set by the other Kinsale exemplars featured in the Bridgestone Guides.

Like the best places, PH is animated, quirky, the sort of dream destination you have to pinch yourself to prove your good luck in being billeted here, at the centre of the action. Mrs Hegarty has energy to burn, and she uses it up in decorating and maintaining this funky house, and in cooking excellent breakfasts in the little breakfast room for her guests. Best of all, PH exudes the sort of grateful satisfaction from its customers that shows you just how happy they are to be here. It is people like the Hegartys and PH who are putting the oomph back into Kinsale.

● **OPEN:** All year, except Christmas
● **ROOMS:** Nine rooms, all en suite
● **PRICE:** €140 per room, including breakfast. Single €80-€120

● **NOTES:** 🖩All major cards accepted. No ♿ access. No dinner. Children welcome. One secure parking space, otherwise public carpark right next door. ✍ Email bookings.

● **DIRECTIONS:**
Coming from Cork, take first left at SuperValu, left at the tourist office, 50m down on right-hand side.

ROCK COTTAGE

Barbara Klotzer
Barnatonicane, Schull
West Cork
℡ **028-35538**
🖷 **028-35538**
🖱 **www.mizen.net/rockcottage**

Barbara Klotzer's elegant house is a by-word for stylish design, meticulous housekeeping, and some very clever, colourful cooking using local foods.

Despite its name, Barbara Klotzer's house, Rock Cottage is, in fact, an elegant Georgian, two-storey, slate-fronted house, dating from 1826, and its swish interior style is modern and European, rather dashing and contemporary, rather than the country-cottagey style, which the name might lead you to expect.

Inside, what you notice first is the meticulous house-keeping, and this level of attention to detail is even more evident in the cooking, at breakfast and at the fine dinners Barbara prepares, intelligent cooking that offers a road map menu of West Cork, menus that use McCarthy's beef from Bantry, Barbara's own lamb from the farm, Rosscarbery pork, Sally Barnes' fantastic smoked fish from Castletownshend; all the great, true tastes of West Cork. Barbara also makes marvellous use of flowers from the garden, both in the rooms and in her cooking. Barbara's self-catering cottage is also a great place to stay.

● **OPEN:** All year
● **ROOMS:** Three rooms and self-catering cottage
● **PRICE:** B&B €55-€65 per person sharing. Single supplement €20.

● **NOTES:** 🖾Visa, Mastercard. Dinner, 7.30pm, book 24hrs ahead, €40, Children over 10 years welcome, working farm. 🖱 Email bookings.

● **DIRECTIONS:**
From Schull, go west towards Goleen. At Toormore turn right onto the R591 towards Durrus. After 2.4km you will see their sign on the left.

SEA VIEW HOUSE HOTEL

Kathleen O'Sullivan
Ballylickey, Bantry
West Cork
✆ **027-50462**
🖷 **027-51555**
🖰 **www.seaviewhousehotel.com**

One of the best-loved coastal hotels you can find in Ireland, Sea View is driven by the dedicated work of Kathleen O'Sullivan and her team.

It says a great deal about Kathleen O'Sullivan's sweet and lovely hotel that it is the first place that comes to mind when you want to take granny and her grandchildren out for Sunday lunch for a treat. That's the style of hotel it is; ageless, charming, with maternal service and well-executed traditional food. Granny will love it. Her grandchildren will love it. And you will love it, for who can resist a meticulously maintained West Cork Victorian house? Not us. And what we admire so much about Ms O'Sullivan and her team is that where most hotels today are obsessed with style, here they are obsessed with service. Whatever it may be that you ask for, nothing is ever too much trouble, and it is done for you with a smile. Isn't that what hotels are supposed to be all about? For us it is, and it explains why Sea View is such a staple of the Bridgestones. After lunch, the kids gambol in the gardens, and you stroll around with granny, everyone very happy.

● **OPEN:** mid Mar-mid Nov
● **ROOMS:** 25 rooms
● **PRICE:** B&B €130-€185 per room

● **NOTES:** All major cards accepted.
Dinner in restaurant 7pm-9pm, Sun lunch (from Easter Sun) and lounge food daily. Dinner €45.
♿ access. Secure parking. 🖰 Email bookings.
Pet friendly.

● **DIRECTIONS:**
On the N71 from Cork, 5km from Bantry and 13km from Glengarriff.

SLIP WAY

Wilmie Owen
The Cove, Baltimore
West Cork
✆ **028-20134**
🖳 **028-20134**
🖰 **www.theslipway.com**

Just across from the water's edge in pretty little Baltimore, Wilmie Owen's sweet B&B is cute, and make sure to book the rooms with the sea views.

For many food lovers, Slip Way was where you stayed when you visited Baltimore to eat at The Customs House, and can we pay tribute to the brilliant cooking of Sue and Ian, and wish them well at their new venture in France. But, even without the CH, Baltimore is still a great destination, and Slip Way a charming place to stay. The rooms are simple, and the rooms at the front with the sea views out over the water are the ones to go for, but their simplicity is apt, appropriate, just right. They aren't small; they are intimate, and that's rather nice. Where Slip Way really comes into its own is at breakfast time. For Wilmie's breakfasts are a delight: velvety, smooth, rich scrambled eggs with smoked salmon; excellent breads and croissants; fine smoky kippers; really good coffee and tea, and more amazing views from the dining room out over the sea. Slip Way is simple and sweet, and great value, and it is the place to lay your head in Baltimore.

● **OPEN:** Mar-Nov
● **ROOMS:** Four rooms, all shower only
● **PRICE:** B&B from €34-€37.50 per person sharing, single rate €55-€70

● **NOTES:** No credit cards.
No dinner.
No ♿ access.
Not suitable for children under 12yrs

● **DIRECTIONS:**
Travel through Baltimore, to the Cove, and you will see the sign, overlooking the Cove.

CASTLE MURRAY HOUSE HOTEL

Marguerite Howley
Dunkineely
County Donegal
✆ **074-973 7022**
🖰 **www.castlemurray.com**

The archetypal Irish restaurant with rooms powers ahead under owner Marguerite Howley and her young, friendly, hard-working team.

Castle Murray House calls itself an hotel, but the truth of the matter is that it's actually a restaurant with rooms, in which guise it is the archetype of such places in Ireland. The rooms are simple, decorated according to various themes, and they are perfect for helping you to make the most of Marguerite Howley's restaurant, where you will enjoy fine seafood cookery, whilst at the same time swooning over some of the most heavenly views you can enjoy anywhere in Ireland – these views simply have to be seen to be believed.

Remy Dupas has been at the stoves here since 1994, his food a comfortable and comforting modern mix of good ingredients and sympathetic technique: salmon fondue with three sauces; turbot with an oregano crust; grilled Blue Bay lobster; duck with roasted shallots, and a true sense of care and creativity from the kitchen is evident in every dish sent out. Castle Murray delivers the goods.

- **OPEN:** All year
- **ROOMS:** Ten rooms
- **PRICE:** B&B €60-€65 per person sharing. Single €80-90

- **NOTES:** 📼Visa, Mastercard.
Restaurant open 7pm-9.30pm Mon-Sat; 1.30pm-3.30pm, 6.30pm-8.30pm Sun; Dinner €46, Sun Lunch €26-30
No ♿ access. Children welcome. Pet friendly.
🖰 Email bookings.

- **DIRECTIONS:**
Castle Murray is signposted just west of Dunkineely.

10 PLACES
WITH GREAT STYLE

1

THE CLARENCE
DUBLIN, Co DUBLIN

2

COAST TOWNHOUSE
TRAMORE, Co WATERFORD

3

GREEN GATE
ARDARA, Co DONEGAL

4

DOLPHIN BEACH
CLIFDEN, Co GALWAY

5

MARLAGH LODGE
BALLYMENA, Co ANTRIM

6

MOSSIE'S
ADRIGOLE, Co CORK

7

OLD GROUND HOTEL
ENNIS, Co CLARE

8

SHELBURNE LODGE
KENMARE, Co KERRY

9

TANNERY TOWNHOUSE
DUNGARVAN, Co WATERFORD

10

WATERSLADE
TUAM, Co GALWAY

COXTOWN MANOR

Eduard Dewael
Laghey
County Donegal
☎ **074-973 4574**
🖨 **074-973 4576**
🖰 **www.coxtownmanor.com**

Ed Dewael's Coxtown
Manor has a secret sur-
prise – one of the most
original Irish breakfasts.

Tired of "The Full Irish", or "The Full Catastrophe", as the
great Irish breakfast should be known? Okay then, take
yourself off to Eduard Dewael's lovely ivy-clad house,
Coxtown Manor, a few miles from Laghey and close to
Bridgetown. At breakfast, ask for the Belgian fry. When it
comes, this is two pieces of splendid bacon set gently
amidst the lightest, fluffiest omelette you can find. And it
is a pure treat, bacon and eggs re-thought, and better than
ever, light and soulful.

That's a gesture typical of Coxtown. Where so many
country houses are clichés, Coxtown is sophisticated,
original, relaxing and unstuffy. The cooking at dinner is
very fine – trio of shellfish is lobster, shrimp and crab;
excellent Thornhill duck with pear; superb Belgian chocolate mousse. The crowd are as cosmopolitan as all get
out, save that there are too few locals, and the rooms –
in particular the newer courtyard rooms – are splendid.

● **OPEN:** mid Feb-end October
● **ROOMS:** Ten rooms
● **PRICE:** B&B €59-€116 per person sharing, depend-
ing on room and season. Single rooms €99-€119

● **NOTES:** 🖬 Visa, Access, Amex, Laser.
Restaurant open Tue-Sat, Dinner, 7pm-9pm.
Children welcome - family rooms. Gourmet breaks
available, dinner plus B&B quoted.

● **DIRECTIONS:**
Look for their sign on the N15 between Ballyshannon
and Donegal, turning just before the Esso station.

GREEN GATE

Paul Chatenoud
Ardvally
Ardara
County Donegal
℅ 074-954 1546
🖰 www.thegreengate-ireland.com

Paul Chatenoud's iconic collection of low cottages isn't for all, but it may well be your spirit's new home.

"Amazing place to stay and fantastic host in Paul Chatenoud... is in our top five". Well, thank you Alistair and Sonja ("fanatical Bridgestone Guide followers") for a sharp thumb-nail assessment of Paul Chatenoud's The Green Gate, that shows above all just how mesmeric this simple collection of low, whitewashed, ancient old stone cottages can be for the first time visitor. If you need the deep-pile 5-star stuff, then the GG is not for you. If you are, instead, seeking something of the spirit of Donegal, if you are hunting what H.V. Morton described as "This light that turns Donegal into a poem for an hour, or for only a second is a terrible and disturbing thing", then you may very well find it here, high on the hill above Ardara, looking down to the sea and feeling like a romantic hero or heroine. M. Chatenoud looks after you with Gallic sincerity and a wistfulness that is totally engaging, and he is a man in tune with that "terrible and disturbing" beauty.

● **OPEN:** All year
● **ROOMS:** Four rooms, all en suite
● **PRICE:** €35 per person

● **NOTES:** No dinner.
No credit cards accepted.
♿ access.
Private parking.
Recommended for families.

● **DIRECTIONS:**
1.5km east of Ardara, way, way up the hill, and signposted from the road.

THE MILL

Derek and Susan Alcorn
Figart, Dunfanaghy
County Donegal
✆ **074-913 6985**
🖨 **074-913 6985**
🖰 **www.themillrestaurant.com**

No one who stays at Derek and Susan Alcorn's The Mill wants to leave this peaceful piece of paradise.

We noted last year that when the McKenna tribe had to move on from The Mill, a gorgeous Edwardian lakeside house that was originally the studio of the watercolourist Frank Eggington, after a single night's residence, that the children and their mother staged a small revolt and smouldered menacingly in the car as the father drove on to the next destination. "Can we get a new Dad, Mum?" Mother and children aren't alone. The wistfulness that is evident in readers' letters about this singular place is palpable, touching, scary: "Cosy drinks by the fire before dinner and coffee in the conservatory afterwards...." wrote one correspondent, and that sums up exactly why The Mill is so good; you don't want to leave it. You want to have cosy drinks by the fire tomorrow night and coffee in the conservatory after one of Derek Alcorn's superb dinners. And the next night. And the next. Like the best places, The Mill is not just home from home: it's home.

● **OPEN:** Easter-Hallowe'en, open every night
● **ROOMS:** Six rooms
● **PRICE:** B&B €85 per room. Single supplement €55

● **NOTES:** 🖳Visa, Mastercard, Amex.
Restaurant open Tue-Sun, dinner, €38.
No wheelchair access. Children welcome - children's menu, travel cot, babysitting if needed.
🖰 Email bookings.

● **DIRECTIONS:**
From L'kenny, take N56 through Dunfanaghy. The Mill is 1km past the village, on the right, beside the lake.

RATHMULLAN HOUSE

The Wheeler family
Lough Swilly
Rathmullan
County Donegal
℗ **074-915 8188**
🖷 **074-915 8200**
🖑 **www.rathmullanhouse.com**

Peace and harmony and lovely food and great wines and an idyllic location and that's Rathmullan House.

If Rathmullan has a secret that explains its special nature, it's not simply that it is a solid and comfortable Georgian mansion close enough to the sea that Andrew Flintoff could throw a stone into the water. It's the fact that the Wheeler family and their crew are supporters of the Slow Food movement that makes everything chime so appositely here: they express their philosophy of consideration and bio-diversity through what they cook, and how they act, and how they treat their guests. Charm, courtesy and timelessness are their tenets, and along with Peter Cheesman's fantastic cooking, it adds up to a formidable cocktail of delights. That cooking is really special, right from his signature assiette of crab – a dish he does better than anyone else – through beetroot and lamb shank terrine to Mossbrook belly of pork with colcannon and on into desserts like chocolate and buttermilk cake and a great traditional Bakewell. Excellent value.

● **OPEN:** Open all year, apart from mid Jan-mid Feb.
● **ROOMS:** 19 rooms
● **PRICE:** €85-€130 per person + 10% service charge.

● **NOTES:** 🖻All major cards accepted. ♿ access. Swimming pool. Rates available for longer stays, and mid-week and weekend in low season.
🖑 Email bookings.

● **DIRECTIONS:**
From Rathmullan, left at Mace store, follow the road past the Catholic Church, then past big black gates. Rathmullan House is at the end of this avenue.

ABERDEEN LODGE

Pat Halpin
53-55 Park Avenue
Ballsbridge, Dublin 4
✆ **01-283 8155**
🖷 **01-283 7877**
🖰 **www.halpinsprivatehotels.com**

Pat Halpin's houses are amongst the city's finest places to stay, and amongst the least well-known.

Pat Halpin is one of those quiet men of excellence to whom few people pay much attention. His customers pay him a great deal of attention, of course, for they know he is the guy who motivates his staff and who, thereby, is responsible for having the best crews in the city. And his staff pay him attention, for they know getting things right is the mantra of Aberdeen Lodge.

But Mr Halpin is a figure of such precise excellence that he deserves further attention. He should be in the media as an example of just how you run private accommodation that enshrines superb standards. He should be written about as a chap who restores and maintains Victorian housing stock to meticulous standards, as he does at Aberdeen Lodge and Merrion Hall. He should be showered with tourism awards, an exemplar of world-class standards for travellers, which also have unique characteristics. He gets none of these, but he gets our award.

- **OPEN:** All year
- **ROOMS:** 17 rooms, including two suites
- **PRICE:** €65-€90 per person sharing, €99-€120 single

- **NOTES:** Light "drawing room" menu, €8-€15 per course, extensive wine list.
Secure parking. Wheelchair access.
🖰 Email bookings.
Children - not suitable for children under 7yrs.

- **DIRECTIONS:**
Just down from the Sydney Parade DART station. Park Avenue runs parallel with Merrion Road & Strand Road.

BEWLEY'S BALLSBRIDGE

Carol Burke (General Manager)
Merrion Road
Ballsbridge, Dublin 4
✆ **01-668 1111**
🖷 **01-668 1999**
🖱 **www.bewleyshotels.com**

The combination of value for money in Bewley's and great food in O'Connell's restaurant is only mighty.

This is the way it is: if we have to travel to Dublin with the family, we stay in Bewley's Ballsbridge. Our friends and their families, travelling to Dublin, stay in BB. Our mates who don't have kids but who have to travel to Dublin stay at BB. Why? Value for money, of course, because we can all stay here without credit card meltdown, and Dublin prices have become scary. And, the kingpin: BB has O'Connell's restaurant, and O'Connell's restaurant is one of the finest in the city, and offers what is unquestionably the best value in the city. Our tribe love the room and the food, the way they are looked after, the little desserts which means that they get two puddings each at the end of dinner. The exhausted McKenna parents love it because the food is glorious and because the McKenna children love it. The rooms are comfy, with space for us all, and the combination of value for money and glorious cooking in O'Connell's Restaurant simply can't be beaten in Dublin.

● **OPEN:** All year, except Christmas
● **ROOMS:** 304 rooms
● **PRICE:** €99 per room

● **NOTES:** 🖃All major cards accepted.
♿ access. Children welcome – large basement drawing room downstairs.
O'Connell's restaurant, dinner from €27.50.
Secure parking.

● **DIRECTIONS:**
On the corner of the Merrion Road, and Simmonscourt Road, adjacent to the Four Seasons Hotel and the RDS.

THE CLARENCE

Oliver Sevestre
6-8 Wellington Quay
Dublin 2
✆ **01-407 0800**
🖷 **01-407 0820**
🖑 **www.theclarence.ie**

There have been significant management and kitchen changes in The
Clarence, but this agelessly stylish
hotel remains an ace place to stay.

That great chef, Antony Ely, has moved on from the Tea
Room restaurant in The Clarence, and the owners have
bought the next-door building with a view to extending
the hotel. A new head chef, Fred Corvonnier, and a new
manager have arrived, and whilst there has been some
flux, we are such admirers of the style of the Clarence
that the hotel remains one of the great destinations. "The
style is genuinely timeless", we noted on our last visit,
"indeed, age seems to make it even better, because it
functions outside of time". That is a magnificent achieve-
ment in design terms, and makes The Clarence lush, tactile, unique, a place it is always a pleasure to return to,
even with the high cost of staying here. The staff are international cool, which is fine if you like international cool,
and we don't, frankly. Breakfasts in the past have been
superb, but kitchen changes meant our last effort was far
from the stratosphere. Great place, and work in progress.

● **OPEN:** All year
● **ROOMS:** 49 rooms, incl penthouse & suites
● **PRICE:** €340-€750 per room, penthouse €2,500,
excluding breakfast.

● **NOTES:** All major credit cards accepted.
Dinner from €55. ♿ access. Valet parking.
Children welcome.

● **DIRECTIONS:**
Overlooking the River Liffey, on the South side, approximately 150 metres up from the Ha'penny Bridge. 30-45
minutes' drive from Dublin airport.

GRAFTON HOUSE

Jay Bourke & Eoin Foyle
Great George's Street
Dublin 2
℡ **01-679 2041**
🖨 **01-677 9715**
🖱 **www.graftonguesthouse.com**

Budget-priced accommodation in Dublin is usually dire, but Grafton House has tons of potential.

Grafton House is a little-known George's Street outpost of the Jay Bourke and Eoin Foyle empire, and is also a work in progress. Housed in the corner of the gorgeous red-brick complex of the South Great George's Street Market, it was always a cut-price accommodation address. We have decided to include it here for two reasons; firstly, it offers a good place to stay in the centre of the city with a good breakfast at a very keen price. Secondly, we hope that by drawing attention to it that B&F will get on with refurbishing more of the rooms, and bringing them up to spec, all the while keeping prices low, of course. What sets GH apart from other budget places is that service is better, and public spaces are much, much better. The rooms that have had the most work done are good, but others can be small and poky, particularly if you are a single. This could be one of the jewels in the expanding B&F empire, and for now it's a good, safe bet.

- **OPEN:** All year, except 21 Dec-30 Dec
- **ROOMS:** 17 rooms
- **PRICE:** from €50 per person sharing, single €60

- **NOTES:** 💳 All major cards accepted.
No restaurant.
Street parking.
Not recommended for children.
🖱 On-line bookings.

- **DIRECTIONS:**
In the very centre of Dublin, three blocks from Grafton Street.

MARBLE HALL

Shelagh Conway
81 Marlborough Road
Donnybrook
Dublin 4
℡ **01-497 7350**
🖱 **www.marblehall.net**

Shelagh Conway's hand-
some house is amongst the
most perfect B&B's you can
find anywhere in Ireland.

The most discreet city B&B is a fine Georgian house
between Donnybrook and Ranelagh in blue-chip south
Dublin. In Marble Hall, Shelagh Conway runs a house that,
we noted on our last visit, "lifts your spirits". It is the
most perfect Georgian minimalism, sparsely and appositely decorated, everything focused on comfort, with
meticulous housekeeping that make sure everything is
gleaming. Breakfast, we scribbled on our menu, was
"amongst the best of all breakfasts, meticulously executed and meticulously described". Ms Conway, for example,
serves Atlantic smoked salmon in scrambled eggs, and
that is what you get; small slivers of fine fish stirred
through the creamy, dreamy eggs, so it is fish in eggs, and
it is sublime. Cashel Blue pancakes with bacon are just as
good, the poached fruits and the breads are benchmark,
the silver tea and coffee pots gleam. Stay for a night in
Marble Hall, and you will feel reborn, your spirits lifted.

- ● **OPEN:** All year
- ● **ROOMS:** Three rooms
- ● **PRICE:** B&B €50 per person sharing

- ● **NOTES:** 🖵No cards accepted.
Not suitable for children. No dinner.
Secure parking. 🖱 Email bookings.

- ● **DIRECTIONS:**
Marlborough Road runs between Ranelagh and
Donnybrook villages. Marble Hall is on the right-hand
side, near the top of the road, driving from
Donnybrook.

MERRION HALL

54-56 Merrion Road
Ballsbridge
Dublin 4
℡ **01-668 1426**
🖰 **www.halpinsprivatehotels.com**

Brilliant service from the best staff in Dublin is the trademark of Pat Halpin's Dublin addresses.

It seems curious to have written it twice about two Dublin destinations, but we noted after our last stay in Merrion Hall that "To walk into the beautiful breakfast room first thing in the morning is to have your spirits lifted".

And, in some ways, that is probably exactly what we are looking for in the Bridgestone Guides; places that transcend your mood; churches of hospitality; tabernacles of good times. We don't want places that keep your feet on the ground: we want places that lift you up where you belong. How can they achieve it? Simple, for we noted that in Merrion Hall, "Mind you, chances are the staff will have done that already". One greeting from these young guys and girls and you are ready to face the day, and we further wrote that "We reckon Pat Halpin has the best crews in Dublin, and if you become a regular at MH, you simply won't stay anywhere else". And that's the truth.

- **OPEN:** All year
- **ROOMS:** 28 rooms, including eight suites
- **PRICE:** €65-€90 per person sharing, €99-€120 single, suite supplement €50

- **NOTES:** Light 'drawing room' menu, €8-€15 per course, extensive wine list. Secure parking.
♿ access. 🖰 Email bookings.
Not suitable for children under 7 years old.

- **DIRECTIONS:**
Ballsbridge is located south of the city centre and Merrion Hall is just opposite the Four Seasons Hotel.

THE MORRISON

Andrew O'Neill
Ormond Quay
Dublin 1
✆ **01-887 2400**
🖷 **01-874 4039**
🖳 **www.morrisonhotel.ie**

J-M Poulot has moved on from the kitchens of The Morrison, but this slick hotel remains a great, groovy destination at the heart of the city.

The Morrison has had significant changes in its kitchens, with the departure of that wonderful cook, Jean-Michel Poulot, who actually opened The Morrison several years back with Hugh O'Regan and Turlough McNamara and John Rocha. But whilst the restaurant will have a period of flux and consolidation, the style template created by John Rocha remains one of the most pleasing and tactile that one can find anywhere in Dublin city, and as such it makes for a special place to stay.

Rocha was quoted a few years back, in regard to his own house, as saying that it is important to get things right at the start, because then they don't need to be changed. That is true of The Morrison: this is a classic design template which seems to get better with time – the same is true of its neighbour, The Clarence. We love the chocolate throws, the dark timber, the lavish scale of the public space, the sexy intimacy of the bars, and it's good value.

● **OPEN:** All year, except 25-26 Dec
● **ROOMS:** 90 rooms and suites, incl penthouse
● **PRICE:** From €270-€310 per room. Supplements apply for suites and superior rooms.

● **NOTES:** 💳All major cards accepted.
Halo Restaurant and Cafe Bar open daily. Lobo, late night club open till 3am. Lunch €30, Dinner €65.
♿ access. Children welcome. Parking rate offered in Jervis St Car Park. 🖳 Email bookings.

● **DIRECTIONS:**
On the north side of the river, near the Millennium Bridge.

THE RED BANK LODGE

Terry McCoy
5-7 Church Street, Skerries
County Dublin
℡ **01-849 1005**
🖷 **01-849 1598**
🖱 **www.redbank.ie**

Some of the best fish cookery you will find is Terry McCoy's secret in The Red Bank: book a room and make the most of a trip north to Skerries.

Terry McCoy's Red Bank restaurant remains a north Dublin destination – indeed a North Dublin institution – thanks to some truly fine, spirited fish cookery. And Mr McCoy's development over the course of the last few years of no fewer than 18 rooms for guests shows that there is energetic, ambitious young blood coursing in this chef's veins. The rooms are as professionally accomplished as everything else in this admirable and hospitable operation, quietly comfortable, with a classless and an ageless style that matches McCoy's own youthful métier. This isn't bling-bling territory: this is an older, graceful, subtle style of comfort and decoration that suits the style of this venerable fish restaurant.

North County Dublin has changed so radically in the last decade, and has so many stressed young workers with kids and big mortgages, that a night away for two at The Red Bank is the hottest ticket north of the River Liffey.

● **OPEN:** All year
● **ROOMS:** 18 rooms, all en suite
● **PRICE:** From €60 per person sharing, single rate from €75

● **NOTES:** All major cards accepted. Restaurant open for dinner (from €45-€48) and Sunday lunch. Special offers, dinner B&B. Check website. On-street parking. Children under 5 free. ♿ access. 🖱 On-line bookings.

● **DIRECTIONS:**
The guesthouse is on the sea front at Skerries.

BALLYNAHINCH CASTLE

Patrick O'Flaherty
Ballinafad, Recess, Connemara
County Galway
℡ **095-31006**
🖷 **095-31006**
🖰 **www.ballynahinch-castle.com**

The ace Ballynahinch Castle is almost certainly the most popular destination in all of Ireland.

The BC – Ballynahich Castle – is really the BFG – the Big Friendly Giant. From the outside, Ballynahinch can look imposing and massive and grandiose, the sort of Citizen Kane statement of wealth and power that is a testament to egotism and megalomania.

But, inside, manager Patrick O'Flaherty and his team have created an oasis that is all about service and satisfaction, and in proving themselves to be dedicated to their task, they have created what is almost certainly the most popular and most admired destination in Ireland. Right from the moment you walk in the door and see the fire blazing in front of the big leather couch and see the fishing rods standing to attention in the hallway, Ballynahinch has you, and there is no escape other than to surrender to its charms. The cooking is great, the grounds are superlative, and young and old, sporty and not-so-sporty, rich and not-so-rich all love Ballynahinch, Connemara's fine BFG.

- ● **OPEN:** All year, except Feb
- ● **ROOMS:** 40 rooms, including three suites
- ● **PRICE:** €95-€200 per person sharing, single supplement €30

- ● **NOTES:** 🖃All major cards accepted.
Dinner in restaurant, €49. ♿ access. Children welcome. 3-4 day breaks, special rates incl. dinner. See website.
🖰 Email bookings.

- ● **DIRECTIONS:**
From Galway, take signs for Clifden (N59). At Recess, and you will begin to see their signs.

DELPHI LODGE

Peter Mantle
Leenane, Connemara
County Galway
✆ **095-42222**
🖷 **095-42296**
🖱 **www.delphilodge.ie**

The one and only Delphi is so elemental and so archetypal that it feels like something out of a dream when you arrive here. Don't worry: it's real.

For many travellers, arriving at Delphi means arriving at the destination of your dreams: the lake stretching out from the front of the gracious and beautifully sited old country house, the awe-inspiring location swaddled deep in the embrace of the Partry Mountains, in mystical Connemara. And, with the prospect of some good fishin' and huntin' to be had if that's your sporting bag, then things seem set for the time of your life. It feels so perfect that it feels like a film location. Except that it's real.

Renowned as a destination for fishermen and hunters, Delphi nevertheless has the sort of graceful, timeless luxury that appeals to everyone: it's not just toys for boys, this is also a house that women love. Food lovers, meantime, expectantly wait to see just what delights Delphi chef Cliodna O'Donogue has cooked up for the table that evening. Great wines from a great cellar at great prices, excellent company, and an all-round civilised place.

- **OPEN:** Mid Jan-mid Dec
- **ROOMS:** 12 rooms, all en suite (seven with lake view)
- **PRICE:** €77-€99 standard room.
Upgrade to lake view room, €22-€30. Single supplement €30

- **NOTES:** Visa & Mastercard. Dinner at 8pm, communal table €49. Limited ♿ access. Secure parking. Young children discouraged. 🖱 Email bookings.

- **DIRECTIONS:**
1km northwest of Leenane on the Louisburgh road. In woods on left about half mile after the Mountain Spa.

DEVON DELL

Berna Kelly
47 Devon Park
Lower Salthill, Galway city
℡ 091-528306
🖱 www.devondell.com

The breakfast table at Berna Kelly's modest Devon Dell is one of the nation's finest, a feast of truly operatic proportions, and utter deliciousness.

Devon Dell is a modest wee house, set at the rere of a cul-de-sac, just ten minutes' walk from the centre of Galway. Never mind the modest circumstances: the secret of DD is the outstanding attention to detail Berna Kelly pays to her house, especially to the linens, the napkins and, above all, to the breakfast table: you walk into the breakfast room here, and your heart gladdens to see such care. And such choice! Bowls of fresh fruit. Smoothies. Bircher muesli marinated in fresh orange juice. Yogurts. Breads, Croissants. Juices. Granola. Even the butter is sculpted into tiny little butter balls. "Just like Ballymaloe!" said our critical kids. Yes, just like Ballymaloe. And then fried eggs, scrambled eggs, waffles, sweet pancakes, whatever else your tum can desire.
Devon Dell is one of a declining number of B&B's, where the heart of the house is the heart of the lady of the house, and there is no more generous heart than Berna.

● **OPEN:** Feb-Oct
● **ROOMS:** 2 double rooms, 1 twin & 1 single, en suite
● **PRICE:** €40-€45 per person sharing

● **NOTES:** No credit cards. No ♿ access.
No facilities for very young children.
Street parking just outside. 🖱 Email bookings.

● **DIRECTIONS:**
Find Fr Griffin Rd, and follow to T-junction, where you take left into Lr Salthill rd. After approx 500m, having passed two pubs, take first right. Go 100m to fork in road, take left and very sharp left into cul-de-sac.

DOLPHIN BEACH

**Sinead & Clodagh Foyle
Lower Sky Road, Clifden
Connemara, County Galway**
✆ **095-21204**
🖨 **095-22935**
🖰 **www.dolphinbeachhouse.com**

Everyone loves Dolphin Beach. What's to love? Oh, everything in Sinead and Clodagh's modern house.

"Just to let you know Dolphin Beach was just fabulous (again!) and we didn't want to leave (again!)."
Blimey. Wouldn't you just love to get a letter like that from someone/anyone: "Darling, you were fabulous (again!) and I didn't want to leave (again!)."
Well, that's the sort of critical feedback you get about Sinead and Clodagh Foyle's megatastic operation, this spectacularly fine modern house sitting close to the sea on the spectacular Sky Road as it winds its way at the edge of the Atlantic ocean. DB works because it is elemental: staying here, you can't imagine being anywhere else; at times, you can't believe anywhere else exists. The house is a superb piece of modern design, with rooms wending and weaving into one another, and then it's dinner in the conservatory overlooking the sea – perhaps a dinner of fresh sea bass or some other fine fresh fish cooked by Sinead, and you don't want to leave (again!).

● **OPEN:** All year, except Christmas & new year
● **ROOMS:** Nine rooms, all en suite
● **PRICE:** €65-€80 per person sharing.
Single supplement €20

● **NOTES:** Dinner 7.30pm, €37. Enclosed parking.
Children over 12 welcome. ♿ access.
Day trips organised.

● **DIRECTIONS:**
Take the Sky road out of Clifden, take the lower fork for 2km. It's the house on the sea side. Clifden is approximately 1 hour's drive from Galway.

10 PLACES WITH
GREAT BREAKFASTS

1

BALLYMALOE HOUSE
SHANAGARRY, Co CORK

2

BALLYVOLANE
CASTLELYONS, Co CORK

3

COXTOWN MANOR
LAGHEY, Co DONEGAL

4

CUCINA
KINSALE, Co CORK

5

DEVON DELL
GALWAY, Co GALWAY

6

GLASHA FARMHOUSE
BALLYMACARBRY, Co WATERFORD

7

HANORA'S COTTAGE
NIRE VALLEY, Co WATERFORD

8

IVYLEIGH HOUSE
PORTLAOISE, Co LAOIS

9

KNOCKEVEN
COBH, Co CORK

10

LONGUEVILLE HOUSE
MALLOW, Co CORK

IVERNA COTTAGE

Patricia & William Farrell
Salahoona
Spiddal
County Galway
℡ **091-553762**
🖰 **www.ivernacottage.8m.com**

Patricia Farrell's meticulous Iverna Cottage is a cultured destination amidst a morass of pretentious housing. Breakfasts are amongst the best.

Patricia and William Farrell's Iverna Cottage has the magic. In the morass of undistinguished – and preposterously pretentious – housing that travails the eyesight from Galway to Spiddal, their stone house is demure, pretty, much cared for. Walk inside, and you are in the cultured land of books, of candlelight, of scents, of music, with maybe a glass of wine to share with the hosts. It is such a relaxing place you feel you must have have moved miles from the main road to Galway. But there the road is, still outside. Forget it: you are already someplace else. 'I don't write a breakfast menu, but people can have whatever they want, and they usually have everything!' says Mrs Farrell. So, start with some fruit, then some cereals, then a grand fry-up, or maybe kippers, or poached eggs with spinach. This is one of the best Irish breakfast tables, and the breakfast is as meticulously conceived and executed as the housekeeping and the hospitality. Magic.

● **OPEN:** May-mid Sept
● **ROOMS:** Four rooms, incl two family rooms
● **PRICE:** €40 per person sharing. Single €50-€60.

● **NOTES:** No credit cards. No specified wheelchair access, though a number of wheelchair users have happily negotiated the step into the house. Children welcome, 33% discount, two family rooms. No dinner.
🖰 Email bookings. Pet friendly.

● **DIRECTIONS:**
The house is exactly 1.6km west of Spiddal on the coast road.

KILMURVEY HOUSE

Treasa & Bertie Joyce
Kilmurvey Bay, Inis Mor
Aran Islands, County Galway
℡ **099-61218**
🖷 **099-61397**
🖱 **www.kilmurveyhouse.com**

Put beautiful Kilmurvey Bay together with beautiful Kilmurvey House and you have the perfect Aran Island recipe for the best times imaginable.

Kilmurvey Bay is one of our favourite places to go swimming in Ireland, the sea crystal-clear, the sand mother-of-pearl white, the graceful arc of the beach like some undiscovered Mediterranean secret. Such bliss! What a boon to the traveller, then, that Treasa Joyce's lovely house should be set so close to Kilmurvey Bay, and the pair of them not much more than a few minutes' jaunt by bus up the road from Kilronan.

If Kilmurvey Bay is the Aran Island beach of your dreams, then Kilmurvey House is the Aran Island B&B of your dreams. Mrs Joyce specialises in great housekeeping – make that superlative housekeeping – great domestic cooking with bumper breakfasts, and lovely, comforting dinners for when you get back, sun-scorched, exhausted. And the result is that you are very quickly going to feel like that cat who got the cream. Such great hospitality and such elemental beauty means taking your leave isn't easy.

- **OPEN:** 1 Apr-16 Oct
- **ROOMS:** 12 rooms, all en suite (seven family rooms)
- **PRICE:** €40-€45 per person sharing. Single €50

- **NOTES:** Dinner €30, 7pm, please book in advance. No wheelchair access. Children welcome.
🖱 Email bookings.

- **DIRECTIONS:**
Take boat from Rosaveel in Connemara. When you arrive in Kilronan, the house is a further 7km from the ferry port. On arrival, take one of the tour buses that crowd down at the port.

THE QUAY HOUSE

Paddy & Julia Foyle
Beach Road, Clifden
Connemara, County Galway
℡ **095-21369**
🖷 **095-21608**
🖱 **www.thequayhouse.com**

Unique. Inimitable.
Exceptional. Bring on the
superlatives for the sub-
limely lovely Quay House.

We have been writing about Paddy Foyle and his various
projects for a very long time, admiring the man's icono-
clasm, his good taste in design, his originality and his style,
the way in which his creative talents as a hotelier and
restaurateur are complemented by Julia Foyle's calm gifts
as hostess and co-creator of the magical Quay House.
But, to tell you the truth, you could know this man for a
lifetime, and you still wouldn't be able to fathom the creative energies he can mainline; you still wouldn't be able
to fathom how it is that he sees things the way he does.
Mr Foyle is like Picasso, we think: a great creator, a great
destroyer of cliché, an endless fount of creative endeav-
our. But, of course, the difference is that Mr Foyle is an
exceptionally nice bloke, whereas Picasso was a monster.
And it's because he is such a nice bloke that Quay House
is such an fantastic place to stay, one of the greatest Irish
houses, in every way an exceptional, artistic address.

● **OPEN:** Mid Mar-Early-Nov. Off season by
arrangement.
● **ROOMS:** 14 en suite rooms, including rooms with
kitchens
● **PRICE:** From €140 per room, B&B, €100 single rate

● **NOTES:** 🖃Visa, Mastercard, Laser. No dinner, but
snacks on request. ♿ access. Street parking. Children
welcomed. 🖱 Email bookings.

● **DIRECTIONS:**
Take the N59 from Galway to Clifden. The Quay House
is down on the quays, overlooking the harbour.

RENVYLE

Ronnie Counihan
Letterfrack, Connemara
County Galway
℡ **095-43511**
🖷 **095-43515**
🖱 **www.renvyle.com**

Executive chef Tim O'Sullivan has published a collection of his recipes from Renvyle, proof of the ambition and intent of this West coast escape.

It is proof of their ambition, and their seriousness, that Renvyle should have published a book of recipes by their executive chef, Tim O'Sullivan, entitled *At Home with Renvyle*. For Mr O'Sullivan has been the kitchen kingpin of Renvyle, and a large element of their success in recent years, as this glorious seaside destination has cemented its reputation as one of the foremost escapes in the West of Ireland. That sense of escape is the key to Renvyle: you turn up here and you tune out, as people have done for more than 120 years, and a great service team under manager Ronnie Counihan takes care of everything else. And, after a day spent doing nothing much of anything much, there is the pleasure of Mr O'Sullivan's cooking to enjoy in the grand dining room: crabmeat salad with passionfruit mayonnaise; a superb spicy parsnip soup; turbot with mustard beurre blanc; seared scallops with lime and ginger hollandaise; classic crème brûlée. Sweet, lovely.

● **OPEN:** Feb-Dec
● **ROOMS:** 68 rooms
● **PRICE:** B&B €30-€110 per person sharing. Single supplement €20.50. Look out for offers on their website.

● **NOTES:** All major cards accepted. Restaurant, serving dinner 7pm-9.30pm, €45. Children welcome, many facilities. Full wheelchair access. 🖱 Email bookings.

● **DIRECTIONS:**
The hotel is signposted from Kylemore. At Letterfrack, turn right, and travel 6.5km to hotel gates.

ROSLEAGUE MANOR

Mark Foyle
Letterfrack, Connemara
County Galway
✆ 095-41101
🖰 www.rosleague.com

Mark Foyle's splendid house is one of the great destinations in the West, a place where everything chimes together perfectly to make enchantment.

It is dreamily perfect, Rosleague Manor. Sitting high on the hill overlooking the bay, this pretty pink Regency house is magical, with every element arranged just so. Small wonder, then, that it is the hottest destination for bespoke weddings in the West, for anyone who visualises their perfect day as a dream-like scenario where everything must be picture-postcard perfect is likely to see it all the more clearly when they see themselves and friends and family cavorting in Rosleague. A perfect day.

Making things perfect is the preserve of Mark Foyle, and despite his youth, this charming man has all the capabilities in the world of hospitality that has always characterised the Foyle family. What we like is that everything here is of a piece; food, wines – a great list – ambience, style, comfort, service, value. So don't think you need a wedding invitation to be at Rosleague: it is one of the finest houses in the west, pretty, pink and kind of perfect.

- **OPEN:** Feb-Dec
- **ROOMS:** 16 bedrooms, four suites
- **PRICE:** €85-€125 per person sharing. Single supplement €35.

- **NOTES:** 🖩 All major cards accepted. Restaurant, serving dinner 7pm-9pm, €45. Children welcome. No ♿ access. 🖰 On-line bookings. Rates for dinner + B&B, and off season mid-week rates available on-line.

- **DIRECTIONS:**
Letterfrack is 11km north west of Clifden. Follow the N59. The house overlooks Ballinakill Bay.

SEA MIST HOUSE

Sheila Griffin
Clifden, Connemara
County Galway
✆ **095-21441**
📧 **sgriffin@eircom.net**
🖐 **www.connemara.net/seamist**

Sheila Griffin's Sea Mist is one of the most charming, aesthetically pleasing B&Bs you will find in Ireland.

Sheila Griffin has created one of the most charming B&B's in the town-centre Sea Mist, a grand Victorian house with a pretty garden and a sunshiney conservatory that somehow manages to be in the centre of busy Clifden and yet to give you the feeling that you are in the heart of the glorious wildness of Connemara.

The modus operandi of this artistic house is a dedication to care, and concern for guests' comfort, and to this end Ms Griffin has arranged the house and its furnishings with the eye of the painter she is. It is an aesthetic treat to stay in Sea Mist, to enjoy the tactility and sensuality of the rooms, to be in the lively ambience of the breakfast room on a fine morning, enjoying a fry-up with Des Moran's smashing pork sausages and his excellent white pudding, enjoying some fruits and cereals and cheeses in the company of so many people having a really great time. Sea Mist is consummately relaxing, a truly great destination.

● **OPEN:** All year, except Christmas and midweek Nov-Feb
● **ROOMS:** Four rooms, all en suite
● **PRICE:** €35-€50 per person sharing, single supplement €15-€20

● **NOTES:** 💳 Visa, Mastercard. No dinner. No ♿ access. No facilities for children. Limited enclosed parking.
🖐 On-line bookings.

● **DIRECTIONS:**
Beside the Bank of Ireland, centre of Clifden, veer left from the square, and it's the stone house on the right.

WATERSLADE HOUSE

Adrian & Vicky Brennan
Waterslade Place, Tuam
County Galway
℡ **093-60888**
🖷 **093-60838**
🖰 **www.watersladehouse.com**

Gorgeously romantic rooms are the secret surprise of Adrian and Vicky Brennan's Waterslade, a stylish house right in the centre of Tuam.

A great sense of design style explains why Adrian and Vicky Brennan's restaurant with rooms has been a big hit with all the hip cats of Tuam. These four rooms are amongst the most distinctively and imaginatively styled places to lay your head in the west, a perfect showcase for demonstrating just how good this pair are at decoration, and at getting the very best out of their manor house, just down the hill close by the river in rapidly-changing Tuam. The contemporary use of colour, a splendid bricolage of painted furnishings, the play of light through the shutters, fine slinky bathrooms, all combine to create a great sense of sensuality and tactility: these are seriously romantic rooms and, in combination with the restaurant, they offer an irresistible combination for those who want to make a big night of it. Downstairs, the restaurant offers good comfort food in a lively atmosphere, and Waterslade is a real treat of a destination.

● **OPEN:** All year, except Christmas
● **ROOMS:** Four rooms, all en suite
● **PRICE:** €65, €85 & €100 per room for double occupancy, €50-€85 single.

● **NOTES:** 🖃All major cards accepted.
Restaurant open 5pm-9pm Wed-Sat ('till 9.30pm Sat);
12.30pm-4pm Sun lunch
No ♿ access to rooms.
Children welcome.

● **DIRECTIONS:**
At the bottom of Shop Street in the centre of Tuam.

10 PLACES WITH
GREAT BATHROOMS

1

THE CLARENCE
DUBLIN, Co DUBLIN

2

COAST TOWNHOUSE
TRAMORE, Co WATERFORD

3

DOLPHIN BEACH
CLIFDEN, Co GALWAY

4

EMLAGH HOUSE
DINGLE, Co KERRY

5

KNOCKEVEN
COBH, Co CORK

6

LONGUEVILLE HOUSE
MALLOW, Co CORK

7

MOY HOUSE
LAHINCH, Co CLARE

8

OLD GROUND HOTEL
ENNIS, Co CLARE

9

SHEEN FALLS
KENMARE, Co KERRY

10

WATERSLADE
TUAM, Co GALWAY

THE CAPTAIN'S HOUSE

Jim & Mary Milhench
The Mall, Dingle
County Kerry
☎ 066-915 1531
🖷 066-915 1079
🖰 www.captaindingle.com

Hospitality is a simple, true instinct with Mary Milhench, and it's the animus that makes Jim and Mary's Captain's House such a special place.

With Mary Milhench, hospitality is utterly instinctive. There she is, welcoming you in, sorting you out, chatting away about what you have been up to, and all the while she is making the coffee, slicing some fruit loaf, lathering jam and cream onto scones and, suddenly: hey presto! there is a delicious welcoming treat of a tray of food in front of you before you even know it. Amazing!

Along with Jim Milhench, Mary powers this tiny, intimate house along on a wave of fabulous energy. The housekeeping is superb, the breakfasts sublime, the welcome 24 carat. It's a little prize of a place, a house that Dingle regulars return to time after time, usually requesting the room they stayed in on their last visit. Mr Milhench, by the by, even finds time to run a garden shop, so the horticulturally inclined amongst you should pay a visit there too Jim and Mary are also wise guides to the latest restaurant openings in this busy town, so you will be well sorted.

- **OPEN:** 15 Mar-15 Nov
- **ROOMS:** Eight rooms, one suite, all en suite
- **PRICE:** €45-€50 per person sharing. Single rate €55-€60. Suite €60 per person sharing

- **NOTES:** 🖻Visa, Mastercard, Laser. No meals. No ♿ access. No facilities for children.
🖰 Email bookings.

- **DIRECTIONS:**
Follow signs to Dingle town centre. The Captain's House is 200m on the left, after the first big roundabout.

CARRIG HOUSE

Frank & Mary Slattery
Caragh Lake, Killorglin
County Kerry
℡ **066-976 9100**
🖷 **066-976 9166**
🖱 **www.carrighouse.com**

An superb lakeside location, ambitious cooking and true hospitality make Carrig a hit on the Ring of Kerry.

We have told the story before of how, when we turned up at Carrig House after Frank and Mary Slattery had taken over and renovated and restored this spectacular lakeside house, that we didn't actually recognise it as the same place we had stayed in not so many years before, when it represented the apotheosis of brown design and brown cuisine and brown hospitality.

In retrospect, now that Carrig has begun to win award after award and accolade after accolade, that transformation strikes us as the Slattery's mission statement: they were making Carrig their way, and what they did with an amazing design make-over, they also did with the cooking – this is a seriously creative kitchen team whose classy, modern, ultra-professional cooking is a treat – and with the hospitality, for there are few places that people seem to enjoy as much as they obviously enjoy Carrig House. A transformation, a transfiguration, a triumph.

● **OPEN:** Mar-end Nov
● **ROOMS:** 16 rooms (including two suites)
● **PRICE:** B&B high season €80-€110, low season €65-€85 per person sharing. Single supplement in double room, €50. Twin room €40 per person.

● **NOTES:** 📼 Visa, Mastercard, Diners. ♿ access. Children over 8 years only. Dinner from 6.30pm, €45 per person. Kennel provided for dogs. 🖱 On-line bookings.

● **DIRECTIONS:**
4km from Killorglin turn left to Caragh Lake, then 2.4km turn right at School. The entrance is 1km further.

EMLAGH HOUSE

Marion & Grainne Kavanagh
Dingle
County Kerry
✆ **066-915 2345**
🖷 **066-915 2369**
🖰 **www.emlaghhouse.com**

In Emlagh, everything is the best it can be, and every detail is constantly examined to see how it can be made better: a truly inspiring house.

In the lovely Emlagh House, everything is not simply the best, everything is the best it can be.

The duvets are the best. The crockery is the best. The tea strainers — for goodness sake! — are the best. The power showers are the best, and indeed these are awesomely powerful, so prepare to be blasted out of your lazy Dingle hangover. The CD players in the rooms are superlative Bose, and they even have a stash of CDs you can choose from (including Norah Jones: hmmm, not the best).

Breakfast offers superb treats such as baked eggs with ham and cream and a little light cheese topping, but you have to work hard to drag your gaze away from the glorious views out across the sea. The paintings and etchings they hang by Kerry painters are glorious, and whilst the house is indeed grand, it never feels indulgent or precious. Instead, it feels like someplace special, a house where the evident luxury is put to service to make you feel good.

● **OPEN:** 10 Mar-1 Nov
● **ROOMS:** 10 rooms
● **PRICE:** B&B €80-€130 per person sharing, €40 single supplement

● **NOTES:** 🖬 Visa, Access, Mastercard, Laser.
No dinner. One room fully wheelchair accessible. Private car park. Children under 8 years not encouraged. 🖰 On-line bookings.

● **DIRECTIONS:**
As one drives west towards Dingle, Emlagh House is the first turn left at the entrance to the town.

HAWTHORN HOUSE

Noel & Mary O'Brien
Shelbourne Street, Kenmare
County Kerry
℡ **064-41035**
🖷 **064-41932**
🖱 **www.hawthornhousekenmare.com**

Kenmare is full of distinguished addresses, and Mary O'Brien's Hawthorn House is yet another one of them, a smashing, cosy, fun house.

Mary O'Brien greets one and all who arrive at Hawthorn House as if they were old friends and, indeed, when you stay here, you will be struck by just how many regular return guests the house enjoys. For newcomers, the sense of relaxation, of true hospitality, of having your wishes taken care of even before you express them, is just some sort of bliss. At breakfast-time, the decibel level is always at full pitch, as everyone enjoys super cooking – lovely poached eggs, nice brown bread, good tea and coffee – and another fine day beckons. The craic has begun, and it is 8am!

The air of relaxed comfort that pervades this simple house but very genuine house is always a treat to enjoy, and Hawthorn is a model, modest B&B. Amiable, unpretentious, friendly, fun. What a pleasure to be back with friends and family in this spick and span B&B, right in the heart of pretty Kenmare, Ireland's gastronomic heart.

- ● **OPEN:** All year, except Christmas
- ● **ROOMS:** Eight rooms, en suite
- ● **PRICE:** €40-€45 per person sharing, Single €55

- ● **NOTES:** 🖾 Visa, Mastercard. No dinner.
  No ♿ access. Enclosed private parking.
  Children welcome, babysitting available.
  🖱 Email bookings.

- ● **DIRECTIONS:**
  There are three main streets in Kenmare. Hawthorn House is situated on Shelbourne Street, the quietest of the three.

ISKEROON

Geraldine Burkitt & David Hare
Bunavalla, Caherdaniel
County Kerry
© 066-947 5119
🖳 066-947 5488
🖱 www.iskeroon.com

The wildest, most romantic location, and the most imaginative design, makes Iskeroon a true cult classic.

Geraldine and David's Hare's Iskeroon is, perhaps, the ultimate cult address in Ireland. It's got all the cult characteristics. The location is utterly other-worldly: turn off the Ring of Kerry, take all the turns down a steep hill which descends at a giddy plummet, then drive across a small beach. And then, there it is, looking out over Derrynane harbour, all but invisible from the land: real adventurers, we guess, would arrive here by yacht.

The design of the house, which dates from 1936, seems almost improvised, and indeed it was built without an architect. Geraldine and David complete this special template with a demon eye for detail: Iskeroon is splendidly finished in William Morris colours, with fabrics from Mallorca, and Mediterranean pottery. Above all, Iskeroon doesn't feel like anywhere else: it feels organic, both in its siting, and in its design and colours which are beautiful, and appositely chosen. It's unique, it's the ultimate cult.

● **OPEN:** 1 May-30 Sep
● **ROOMS:** Three rooms, each with private bathroom. Self-catering apartment for two
● **PRICE:** from €140 per room. Single occupancy €100

● **NOTES:** 🖃Visa, Mastercard, Laser. No meals available. No wheelchairs. Not suitable for children.
🖱 Email bookings.

● **DIRECTIONS:**
Find the Scarriff Inn between Waterville and Caherdaniel. Take sign to Bunavalla Pier. At the pier, go through gate marked 'private road', beside beach through pillars.

THE KILLARNEY PARK HOTEL

Padraig & Janet Treacy
Kenmare Place, Killarney
County Kerry
℡ **064-35555**
🖷 **064-35266**
🖰 **www.killarneyparkhotel.ie**

Janet and Padraig Treacy are amongst the most distinguished hoteliers, and the Killarney Park is a gem.

Want to know what is the best-kept secret in Killarney? The quality of food served in the bar of the Killarney Park Hotel. This is where all the food-loving locals go to eat. When our editor, Orla Broderick, was having a few days in Killarney, she came here with husband and baby. "The cooking! And they are so helpful with the baby! It should be in the Bridgestone 100 Best Restaurants!"

But the quality of the food in the bar of the KP is simply emblematic of the stratospheric standards you will encounter in the KP. The rooms are special. The spa is special. The Park restaurant is special. The staff are special. And everything is special because of Padraig and Janet Treacy, who lead this operation from the front, who lead by example. They are driven by a restless urge to improve, and they have never stopped improving, and every day they vow to improve some more. The KP is one of the greatest examples of Irish hospitality, a true star.

● **OPEN:** All year, except Christmas
● **ROOMS:** 71 rooms
● **PRICE:** €265-€400 per room, €365-€750 suites

● **NOTES:** 🖃Visa, Mastercard, Amex, Laser. Restaurant & Bar, Dinner €60. Children welcome, babysitting and facilities available on request. 🖢 access.
🖰 On-line bookings.

● **DIRECTIONS:**
At 1st roundabout in Killarney (coming from Cork), take 1st exit for town centre. At 2nd roundabout take 2nd exit and at 3rd roundabout take 1st exit.

THE PARK HOTEL

Francis & John Brennan
Kenmare
County Kerry
℡ **064-41200**
🖷 **064-41402**
🖱 **www.parkkenmare.com**

The super-stylish, state-of-the-art Samas spa has been attracting a great deal of attention – and an international audience – to Kerry's Park Hotel.

The very grand, state-of-the-art Samas spa has created an international focus of attention in John and Francis Brennan's famous Kenmare hotel, The Park. To give you an idea of the sort of attention to detail that comes naturally to this team, you should note that Samas even has its own soundtrack of music, commissioned and composed specially for the spa, by the former Roxy Music saxophonist, Andy McKay. And jolly good it is, too, a far cry from the vapour of sound that is endemic in so many spas.

But having a top-class international spa is just the latest thing that the Brennan brothers have done. What also continues in The Park is the art of gracious hotel keeping, the running of a top class hotel by a top-class team, people who seem able to read your mind, people who know what you want even before you know it yourself. It's a most gracious, grand address, a reminder of how the great international hotels used to operate in the old days.

● **OPEN:** 18 Apr-30 Nov & 23 Dec-2 Jan. Weekends only in Nov
● **ROOMS:** 46 rooms
● **PRICE:** B&B €166-€228 per person sharing. Suites & de luxe rooms €317-€385. Single €206-€256

● **NOTES:** 🖃All major cards accepted. Restaurant open daily, Dinner from 7pm, €69. ♿ access. Secure parking. Luxury spa. Children under 4 years sharing, complimentary. 🖱 On-line bookings.

● **DIRECTIONS:**
At the top of Kenmare town.

SHEEN FALLS LODGE

Adriaan Bartels
Kenmare
County Kerry
℡ **064-41600**
📠 **064-41386**
🖰 **www.sheenfallslodge.ie**

With manager Adriaan
Bartels leading an ace team,
the luxurious SFL goes
from strength to strength.

One of the best things about Adriaan Bartels and his crack team in Kenmare's luxurious Sheen Falls Lodge is the fact that they always over-deliver. Levels of service in this grand hotel are of stratospheric standards, right across the board, from the first greeting to dinner service to the last farewell. Nothing is taken for granted, nothing is left to chance. The place runs like a Swiss timepiece. And this constant striving means that the SFL always has a living, breathing, moving forward sense about it. Yes it's expensive and grand, but it's not a mausoleum for rich folk, like some other high-roller places. It's a place where good people do good work, and where those good people try every year to get better and better.

This animus keeps this beautiful place ticking at top notch, an hotel where the art of hospitality is practiced at a pitch-perfect level. Cooking, design, and comfort are all aligned in what is an almost Mozartian perfection.

● **OPEN:** First Fri in Feb-2 Jan
● **ROOMS:** 66 rooms
● **PRICE:** €280-€425 per room. Supplements apply for superior rooms and suites.

● **NOTES:** 💳All major cards accepted.
Dinner, €69. ♿ access. Children welcome, 'kiddies club'.
Two thatched cottages for rental, exclusively catered for.
🖰 On-line bookings.

● **DIRECTIONS:**
Heading towards Glengarriff, the hotel is on the first turn left after the suspension bridge.

SHELBURNE LODGE

Tom & Maura Foley O'Connell
Killowen, Cork Road
Kenmare, County Kerry
✆ **064-41013**
🖨 **064-42135**

No other house feels like Maura Foley's glorious, glamorous Shelburne, one of the great destinations.

One of the best times to enjoy Shelburne Lodge is just at that point when you come in, after a long and tiring day's leisure, and find yourself drawn in from the hallway by a crackling open fire. Light. Heat. Comfort. Aah!

Perhaps that's why, next morning, when everyone comes downstairs, they are all smiling. Or perhaps we're all smiling in anticipation of Maura Foley's breakfast. For it is here that we see all the skills of a chef who has been at the top of her game for years. Expect little cheffy touches, like a subtle hint of ginger in the syrup that dresses fresh pineapple and strawberries, or a pot of whiskey cream for your porridge, or a perfect omelette, or some sparkling fresh fish. Shelburne combines a rigorous professionalism, with a spontaneous sense of care. Senga O'Connell is the sweetest, most genuine young host, and Tom O'Connell is the perfect, kind foil to Maura's dazzling competence. Together the Foleys make a house that is extra-special.

● **OPEN:** Mar-mid Dec
● **ROOMS:** Seven rooms, all en suite
● **PRICE:** €100-€145 per room. Single €75-€90

● **NOTES:** 💳Visa, Mastercard.
No restaurant (good restaurants locally). Enclosed car parking. No ♿ access. Low season special rates available. Children welcome, high chair, cot.

● **DIRECTIONS:**
300m from Kenmare centre, across from the golf course on the Cork road. Kenmare is 35 miles from Kerry airport, 56km from Cork airport.

ZUNI

**Paul & Paula Byrne, Sandra &
Alan McDonald
26 Patrick St, Kilkenny**
© **056-772 3999**
🖷 **056-775 6400**
🖰 **www.zuni.ie**

Zuni's owners exhibit the necessary self-criticism of the very best hoteliers, so this hot address just gets even better and better as time goes by.

Zuni has been the red hot destination in Kilkenny over the last few years, and its restaurant, in particular, has gotten better and better in recent years, making it one of the most enjoyable and exciting places to eat, not just in Kilkenny, but indeed anywhere in Ireland.
But Zuni is also a small boutique hotel in the centre of the city, where 13 rooms have been sculpted out of this old, Kilkenny address with great skill. Selling the rooms at very fair prices has meant that a great many people heading to Kilkenny for the weekend will first of all book a room and a table here, and use Zuni as their base for a fun escape from Dublin. And, just to show that they can master all the arts, Zuni has a very fine bar, the sort of softly-lit space with great armchairs that could be in any major metropolis. And that is the secret of Zuni: it feels metropolitan. It makes one feel glam, and at the centre of the action. And that is the great feat Zuni has achieved.

● **OPEN:** All year, except Christmas
● **ROOMS:** 13 rooms, all en suite
● **PRICE:** €50-€90 per person sharing

● **NOTES:** 🖃 Visa, Access, Amex, Laser.
Restaurant open for dinner Mon-Sun. ♿ access. Enclosed private parking at rear. Children welcome.
🖰 On-line bookings.

● **DIRECTIONS:**
Located in the city centre, on Patrick Street, which is round the corner from Kilkenny Castle. Take M50 from Dublin airport. Take N7 southbound direct to Kilkenny.

IVYLEIGH HOUSE

Dinah & Jerry Campion
Bank Place
Portlaoise, County Laois
✆ **0502-22081**
🗎 **0502-63343**
🕆 **www.ivyleigh.com**

Dinah Campion's meticulous dedication to her calling makes Ivyleigh House one of the most pristine, comfortable addresses to lay your head.

Frette towels. Gilchrist & Soames toiletries. Sumptuous antique beds. Beautifully restored period details. Extraordinary housekeeping. And then there's breakfast: poached plums; prunes and apricots; granola; muesli; melon and orange; Cashel Blue pancakes with mushrooms and tomatoes; fresh white bread; fresh brown bread; tea in a glistening silver pot.

Dinah Campion's smart town house, close to the centre of Portlaoise, is a special place, thanks to the endless efforts of the hostess to make it special. Mrs Campion's eye for detail is rigorous, almost ruthless. Everything she can do to make something special, then she will do it. But, the rub is that she will do it better than anyone. She is a driven person, a meticulous creator of comfort. Merely reciting the breakfast ingredients can't do justice to the originality and intricacy of her cooking, for those Cashel Blue breakfast pancakes are truly special. A great address.

● **OPEN:** All year, except Christmas
● **ROOMS:** Four rooms, all en suite
● **PRICE:** €62.50 per person sharing. Single in double/twin €75, single room €70

● **NOTES:** No dinner. No ♿ access.
On street car parking. Children over 8 years welcome.
🕆 Email bookings.

● **DIRECTIONS:**
In Portlaoise, follow the sign for multi storey car park. At car park entrance there is a sign with directions for Ivyleigh House.

ROUNDWOOD HOUSE

Frank & Rosemary Kennan
Mountrath
County Laois
✆ **0502-32120**
📠 **0502 32711**
🖱 **www.roundwoodhouse.com**

Frank and Rosemary's Roundwood House is one of the most charming, unpretentious and real of the Irish country houses: prepare to fall in love.

If you have any romance in your soul, if you have any flibbertigibbet faculty in your mindset, then you will surely fall under the spell of Roundwood House.

Abandon critical perspective, for this is not a house to be cool about. It is not a house to analyse, or pontificate over. It's not a house to be indifferent about. It's simply a place to fall in love with, whatever your age, sex, nationality or IQ The cynic in you will be excised, and you will quickly be enthusing to all your new best friends, as you sit and chat and drink with them around the dinner table, agreeing what an amazing place Roundwood House is.

The cold eye which you might cast about the place, and which might remark on the ancien pauvre style and the elegantly distressed furnishings, will be dissolved in the pleasure of Rosemary's splendid cooking, and the irresistible bonhommie this lovely house seems to conjure from out of the ether. Roundwood is an enchantment.

● **OPEN:** All year, except Christmas & 2-31 Jan
● **ROOMS:** 10 rooms, all with private bathrooms
● **PRICE:** €75 per person sharing. Single supplement €25

● **NOTES:** Dinner, 8pm, €45, communal table.
Book by noon. No ♿ access.
Children welcome, high chair, cot, babysitting.
🖱 Email bookings.

● **DIRECTIONS:**
Turn right at traffic lights in Mountrath for Ballyfin, then left onto R440. Travel for 5km on the R440 until you come to the house.

THE COURTHOUSE

Piero & Sandra Melis
Main Street
Kinlough
County Leitrim
✆ **071-984 2391**
🖰 **www.thecourthouserest.com**

Piero Melis' little restaurant with rooms in pretty Kinlough is one of the key addresses in the beautiful, waiting-to-be-discovered, borderlands.

Kinlough, in lovely County Leitrim, is a darling little space with a darling little place – The Courthouse – bidding you to stop, eat and stay the night.

The rooms are simple, as you would expect of a restaurant with rooms run by an Italian proprietor who hails originally from Sardinia. But Piero's restaurant is very fine, a charming space that is comfortable, unpretentious and fun to be in whether you are alone, with a group or with the family. The staff are superb, the sounds are cool, and Mr Melis' cooking eschews any pretensions and heads straight for deliciousness, just as we always hope and expect from the Italian style. Home-made pastas are terrific, meat dishes are absolutely classic, whilst the desserts are splendid and simple, and prices for such good cooking are extremely keen. Don't miss the Sardinian wines imported by Piero, and don't miss this neat little getaway, and its taste of the sublime, in Leitrim.

● **OPEN:** All year except Xmas & two weeks in Nov & Feb
● **ROOMS:** Four rooms
● **PRICE:** B&B €37 per person sharing, €42 single

● **NOTES:** 💳Visa, Access, Mastercard, Laser. ♿ access. Children welcome, but not in the restaurant after 8pm. Dinner 6.30pm-9.30pm, ('till 10pm high summer), €40.

● **DIRECTIONS:**
On the main street in Kinlough, turn off the main Donegal/Sligo road at Bundoran, on the bridge opposite the post office.

HOLLYWELL COUNTRY HOUSE

Rosaleen & Tom Maher
Liberty Hill, Carrick-on-Shannon
County Leitrim
✆ **071-962 1124**
🖷 **071-962 1124**
🖱 **hollywell@esatbiz.com**

The Maher boys are making a splash
with their Oarsman restaurant, whilst
the Maher parents continue to run a
house that is a beacon of hospitality.

The Maher family's magical way with hospitality has
extended its capable tentacles over the bridge and into
Carrick-on-Shannon itself, as Tom and Rosaleen Maher's
boys, Conor and Ronan, have made an enormous success
of The Oarsman pub in the centre of the town. To see
these chaps at work, to see the care they lavish on their
customers and their cooking, is to see a family gene that
has hospitality stamped all over it: they are peas from the
pod of a family who personify all the good things of hospitality: civility, hard work, respect, true service, a desire
to please, a striving for excellence.

And they learnt it all from their folks, who run what is
one of the loveliest addresses in the North West.
Hollywell is pretty, dignified, companionable, because it is
simply so expertly run by the Mahers. It's a cosy house,
extremely relaxing, it has delicious cooking, and there is
nothing about this area that the Mahers do not know.

● **OPEN:** 1 Mar-31 Oct
● **ROOMS:** Four rooms, all en suite
● **PRICE:** €50-€70 per person sharing. Single supple-
ment €20-€30

● **NOTES:** No dinner. Enclosed car park.
No ♿ access. Children over 12 years welcome.
🖱 Email bookings.

● **DIRECTIONS:**
From Carrick-on-Shannon, cross the bridge,
keep left at Gings pub. The entrance to Hollywell is on
the left.

THE MUSTARD SEED

Daniel Mullane
Echo Lodge, Ballingarry
County Limerick
℗ **069-68508**
🖨 **069-68511**
🖰 **www.mustardseed.ie**

Dan Mullane is one of the most successful hosts in Ireland, thanks to an ability to do everything superbly.

Whatever Dan Mullane does, he does it to the accompaniment of great success.

For ten years he ran the Mustard Seed with great success in Adare, before moving his restaurant here to a fine house which now has no fewer than eighteen glamorous, luxurious rooms. And for ten years now he has enjoyed great success in Echo Lodge.

How does he do it? Simple. He looks after people. He provides comfort and comforting food. He knows what you want better than you know yourself. In that regard, he is the quintessential host. But, what Mr Mullane also enjoys is the ability to create the perfect space in which people really enjoy themselves, and the sound of people enjoying themselves is very much the soundtrack to Mr Mullane's success. Echo Lodge is a rocking busy restaurant and country house, and its attractions are almost addictive: given a taste, you immediately crave more.

● **OPEN:** All year, except first two weeks in Feb
● **ROOMS:** 16 rooms, including three suites
● **PRICE:** €90-€150 per person sharing. Single supplement €20-40, triple room supplement €60

● **NOTES:** 💳 Visa, Mastercard, Access.
Dinner €35-€54. ♿ access. House not suitable for young children. 🖰 On-line bookings.
Pets by arrangement only.

● **DIRECTIONS:**
Take the Killarney road from Adare, 500m until you reach first turning off to the left, signed for Ballingarry.

GHAN HOUSE

Paul Carroll
Carlingford
County Louth
℡ **042-937 3682**
🖷 **042-937 3772**
🖱 **www.ghanhouse.com**

Paul Carroll has made
Ghan House into one of the
best and hottest addresses
on the east coast of Ireland.

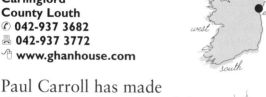

Paul Carroll has made Ghan House into the star of County Louth and the star of sweet little Carlingford, a benchmark address that manages, somehow, to keep on getting better and better. His fame has spread most recently into Northern Ireland, from where the house now pulls in droves of happy travellers to enjoy the comfort of the rooms, the food, and the wines, and a large proportion of weekend guests to beautiful Carlingford are now crossing over the border before arriving at this imposing country house and sitting down in front of the fire with a gin and tonic, perusing the menu.

Mr Carroll's house works because he is such an excellent motivator of his staff, and such a wise student of the arts of hospitality. But Ghan is also blessed to be just on the fringe of Carlingford, one of the most attractive villages in the country and one of the best weekend destinations to escape to, especially when they ban the jetskis.

● **OPEN:** All year, except Christmas & New Year
● **ROOMS:** 12 bedrooms, all en suite
● **PRICE:** €90-€100 per person sharing, single from €70

● **NOTES:** 🖮 Visa, Mastercard, Access, Amex. Restaurant open Fri-Sat, 7pm-9.30pm. Midweek & Sun by arrangement, €47. No wheelchair access. Children welcome. 🖱 Email bookings.

● **DIRECTIONS:**
Approaching from south, Ghan House is 1st driveway on left after 50kph sign on entering Carlingford. 85km from Dublin, 69km from Belfast.

NEWPORT HOUSE

Kieran & Thelma Thompson
Newport
County Mayo
℡ **098-41222**
🖷 **098-41613**
🖱 **www.newporthouse.ie**

Newport House offers one
of the finest country house
experiences in Ireland,
sumptuous in every regard.

Newport is one of those rare houses that manages, seemingly without trying, to weave a spell all around you. The fine big, ivy-clad house just over the bridge as you come into Newport is an enchantment of great service, great classical Irish country house cooking, and a unique, noble atmosphere. It is one of the great country houses, grand, surreal, sophisticated, and quite lovely.

The spell is further intoxicated when we get to dinner-time, and John Gavan's sumptuous cooking: Clew Bay oysters Rockefeller; charcoal-grilled sirloin with red wine butter; pork with white wine, brandy, sage and lemon sauce; sole meunière with hollandaise; strawberry short-bread with raspberry coulis and vanilla sauce. This is classic cooking, cooking that has no need to play with foodie fashions, and it is presented and served in the appropriate manner, with a modest grandeur. Great bedrooms great breakfasts, and altogether a unique experience.

● **OPEN:** 18 Mar-8 Oct
● **ROOMS:** 18 rooms, 16 en suite
● **PRICE:** B&B €108-€162, Single supplement €28, superior room supplement €28. Dinner B&B €166-€221

● **NOTES:** 🖮Visa, Mastercard, Access, Amex. Restaurant open for casual lunch and formal dinner. Dinner €59. Limited wheelchair access. Children welcome, no charge under 2 yrs, 30% reduction under 12 yrs, sharing. 🖱 Email bookings. Pets in courtyard rooms.

● **DIRECTIONS:**
In the centre of the village of Newport, on N59 route.

ROSTURK WOODS

Louisa & Alan Stoney
Mulrany, Westport
County Mayo
☎ **098-36264**
🖰 **www.rosturk-woods.com**

Louisa Stoney is one of the most
super-charged of hostesses, a woman
with boundless energy who manages
to do a million things at any one time.

Rosturk is a lovely house, brightly coloured, gaily decorated, tucked away in the midst of surrounding woods,
and, above all, a place blessed with the flickering light that
bounces off the lapping waters of nearby Clew Bay, a light
that suffuses and animates this lovely place.

Something about Rosturk seems perfectly to capture and
express the wild, seaboard spirit of this adorable part of
Mayo, on the road between Newport and Achill Island.

And, if the house expresses a spirit of place, Louisa
Stoney matches it, every time, with a spirit of wilful determination. For here is one of those women who manages
to do everything, and to do it charmingly and effortlessly;
someone whose animation brings alive the place where
they live and work. She is a true hostess: knowledgeable
about the area and all its diversions and specialities, a
super cook should you ask her to cook dinner, and a free
spirit who makes you feel you are someplace special.

● **OPEN:** Mar-Nov
● **ROOMS:** Three double/twin rooms, all en suite
● **PRICE:** €50 per person sharing, €20 single
supplement

● **NOTES:** No credit cards accepted. Dinner, €38. Self
catering accommodation available. ♿ access in self-catering houses only. Secure parking. Children welcome.
🖰 Email bookings. Pet friendly.

● **DIRECTIONS:**
11km from Newport, heading towards Achill, after you
have crossed Owengrave River, look for their blue sign.

STELLA MARIS

Frances Kelly & Terence McNally
Ballycastle
County Mayo
☏ **096-43322**
🖷 **096-43965**
🖑 **www.StellaMarisIreland.com**

A beautiful place to stay, a super restaurant, and a great buzzy town in the shape of Ballycastle: Stella Maris is at the heart of all the Mayo action.

Stella Maris changed our mind about County Mayo, along with the painter Stuart Shills, whose paintings taught us to look at the wild elements of the Mayo weather in a different light. Shills' paintings seemed to say; feel the texture of the rain, and don't worry about getting wet. Stella Maris seemed to say; enjoy the tactile pleasures of this place, whilst we look after you.

Now, maybe it was because they looked after us so well that we had a rethink about Mayo, which we had always heretofore regarded as being full of unexplored potential. But in Stella Maris, the potential for pleasure is fully explored, thanks to Ms Kelly's smashing cooking, and Mr McNally's laid-back hospitality. The food reads simply – sautéed lambs kidneys; smoked haddock risotto; Mayo lamb with a herb crust; magret of duck with buttered cabbage; glazed lemon tart – but it eats true and tasty, well conceived and cooked, the right food in the right place.

● **OPEN:** Easter-mid-Oct
● **ROOMS:** 11 rooms
● **PRICE:** B&B €90-€150 per person sharing

● **NOTES:** 💳Visa, Mastercard, Access.
♿ access. Limited ability to accommodate young children. Dinner 7pm-9pm (until 10pm weekends), €40. 🖑 Email bookings.

● **DIRECTIONS:**
Go down the hill from Ballycastle, and the Stella Maris is signposted from here. Turn right, it's on the Pier Road, overlooking the sea.

CASTLE LESLIE

Sammy Leslie
Glaslough
County Monaghan
✆ **047-88100**
🖷 **047-88256**
🖰 **www.castleleslie.com**

The scale of the plans for developing Castle Leslie would take your breath away. But have no doubt that this crack crew are more than capable.

Everything in Castle Leslie has always been done on a gargantuan scale, ever since the Leslie family built this colossal Gothic pile aeons ago. Today, the gargantuan, epic scale rests with the development plans, which Sammy Leslie has formulated to turn Castle Leslie into a mega-complex of hospitality.

Already, staff numbers have more than doubled, and nearly 100 people work here now. There are plans to restore the 4-acre walled garden over the next five years, and executive chef Noel McMeel will have his cookery school up and running by the end of the year. The new rooms in the house are finished, and the gate lodge is being developed. It's all happening at breathtaking speed, but Noel McMeel's focus is clear: modern Irish food, with their own and other local ingredients, cooked with sympathy and understanding. Mr McMeel never loses sight of the foundation stone of all hospitality: care for the customer.

● **OPEN:** all year, including Christmas
● **ROOMS:** 20 rooms
● **PRICE:** B&B €135-€185 per person sharing. Dinner B&B €185-€235

● **NOTES:** 🖻 Visa, Mastercard. No wheelchair access. No children under 18 years. Dinner 6pm-9.30pm, €54. Cookery school opening in 2006. 🖰 On-line bookings.

● **DIRECTIONS:**
2 hours from Dublin off the N2. Just under 2 hours from Belfast. Detailed directions can be e-mailed or faxed.

TEMPLE HOUSE

Roderick & Helena Perceval
Ballymote
County Sligo
℡ **071-918 3329**
🖷 **071-918 3808**
🖰 **www.templehouse.ie**

It would take a Tolstoy or a Proust to do justice to the magic that is the Perceval family's Temple House.

Roderick and Helena Perceval have taken on the day-to-day business of running the splendiferous Temple House, but, given that the Percevals have been here since 1665 or thereabouts, the family are well used to succeeding generations taking on the task of running this gargantuan house and its 1,200 acres, complete with walled garden, its lake, its formidable ruins, and its multifarious magic. We don't use that term "magic" lightly, for there really is something special, something otherworldly, something unique about this house. You would need a Tolstoy to do justice to its scale, its strangeness, its wonder. All we can do is to point out that the food is deliciously fantastic, the guests are the sort of folk destined to become your best friends, and the experience of staying here many times over the years only ever makes us want to hurry back one more time for a fix of that magic. Temple House is unlike any other place to stay in Ireland.

● **OPEN:** 1 Apr-30 Nov
● **ROOMS:** Six rooms
● **PRICE:** €65-€85 per person sharing. Single supplement €20.

● **NOTES:** 🖃Visa, Mastercard, Laser.
Dinner, 7.30pm, €42. High tea for children under seven, 6.30pm. No ♿ access. Private parking.
Children welcome, rocking horse.
🖰 Email bookings.

● **DIRECTIONS:**
Signposted off the N17 10km south of the N4 junction.

10 GREAT
COASTAL GETAWAYS

1
DOLPHIN BEACH
CLIFDEN, Co GALWAY

2
GHAN HOUSE
CARLINGFORD, Co LOUTH

3
ISKEROON
CAHERDANIEL, Co KERRY

4
KELLY'S RESORT HOTEL
ROSSLARE, Co WEXFORD

5
THE MILL
DUNFANAGHY, Co DONEGAL

6
QUAY HOUSE
CLIFDEN, Co GALWAY

7
RENVYLE
LETTERFRACK, Co GALWAY

8
ROSSLEAGUE MANOR
LETTERFRACK, Co GALWAY

9
ROSTURK WOODS
NEWPORT, Co MAYO

10
STELLA MARIS
BALLYCASTLE, Co MAYO

395

BAILEY'S

Phil Delaney
Cashel
County Tipperary

Superior Twin

✆ 062-61937
🖷 062-63957
🖰 www.baileys-ireland.com

north
east
west
south

Bailey's is a pretty Georgian town-house right in the centre of newly-peaceful Cashel, from where the noisy lorries are long since departed.

Phil Delaney has been the creator of two addresses in Cashel town, for before he set about the business of refurbishing Bailey's, right in the centre of the town, he established Legends, another B&B close to the Rock of Cashel. Now, almost five years after finishing a lot of painstaking work on Bailey's, this imposing Georgian house, set slightly back from the road, offers excellent accommodation and lovely breakfasts and, a great boon for tired travellers, it also has a restaurant in the basement, imaginatively called The Cellar.

Bailey's has been blessed with the opening of the Cashel by-pass, because heretofore this fine town was on the main N7-N8 Dublin-Cork route, and staying in a room at the front of the house meant that you could not avoid the noise of lorries. That problem has now been solved, so Bailey's makes an ideal address if you are visiting The Rock, and spending time in this compact, energetic town.

● **OPEN:** Open all year, except Christmas & Jan
● **ROOMS:** 19 rooms, all en suite
● **PRICE:** €50-55 per person sharing. Single €55

● **NOTES:** 🖭Visa, Mastercard, Access, Amex.
Fully licensed bar and restaurant, dinner €40.
Access to adjacent leisure facilities, incl pool opening 2006.
🖰 Email bookings.

● **DIRECTIONS:**
In the centre of Cashel, on the main street, on the left-hand side when heading towards Cork.

INCH HOUSE

John & Nora Egan
Thurles
County Tipperary
℅ **0504-51261/51348**
🖷 **0504-51754**
🖰 **www.inchhouse.ie**

A charming, comfortable country house with comfort food and genuine hospitality, the Egan family's Inch House is a key Midlands address.

If there is a signature to Inch House that remains with you after you have left, it is the sheer generosity of the entire crew who run this fine big manor house just a few miles from Thurles.

The rooms are generous in size and very comfortable – and if we mention again the little crucifix above the door of each room it may give you some insight into the unaffected way in which the Egan family run their house. The cooking from Kieran O'Dwyer, who has run the kitchens here since 1996, is a deliciously generous country cooking that makes the restaurant the destination address for miles around: smoked salmon tagliatelle; chicken wrapped in bacon and stuffed with garlic and herbs; entrecote with cracked black pepper – and the dining room is a superbly comfortable, elegant space, both for dinner and breakfast. Put all of the elements together and you understand why Inch is such a local hero, a most generous local hero.

- **OPEN:** All year, except Christmas
- **ROOMS:** Five rooms, all en suite
- **PRICE:** €55 per person sharing, Single €65

- **NOTES:** 🖃All major cards accepted.
Dinner 7pm-9.30pm Tue-Sat, €45-€47.
No ♿ access Children welcome, cot, high chair, babysitting on request. 🖰 Email bookings.

- **DIRECTIONS:**
6.4km from Thurles on the Nenagh road.
Turn off at the Turnpike on the main N8 road, signpost Thurles.

AN BOHREEN

Jim & Ann Mulligan
Killineen West, Dungarvan
County Waterford
℡ **051-291010**
🖷 **051-291011**
🖱 **www.anbohreen.com**

Ann Mulligan's heavenly cooking, and fantastic value for money, make An Bohreen a one-of-a-kind place that should be on everyone's N25 route.

Ann Mulligan's menus in An Bohreen, a single-storey modern home set high on the hill overlooking Dungarvan Bay and the Comeragh mountains, read straightforward enough – Dungarvan Bay fish soup; poached salmon with bohreen sauce, Waterford lamb with mint chutney; chocolate marquise. This modest script doesn't reveal that Mrs Mulligan, an American graduate of the Ballymaloe school, is a seriously gifted cook, but you may gather that fact when you enter the house, as everything here is orientated towards the dining room.

Mrs Mulligan's gift is to bring a touch of magic to the ingredients she sources so carefully, and this expert, professional touch animates her cooking. Dinner, and equally expert breakfasts, gave real frisson to staying in An Bohreen, and the bedrooms are comfortable and elegantly simple places to lay your head. Jim Mulligan knows everything that moves in these parts, especially for golfers.

- **OPEN:** Mar 17- end Oct
- **ROOMS:** Four rooms
- **PRICE:** €37.50-€40 per person sharing. Single €50-€55

- **NOTES:** 🖃Visa, Mastercard, Laser. Dinner 8pm, €36, book by noon. No ♿ access. Secure parking. No children under 12 years. 🖱 Email bookings.

- **DIRECTIONS:**
Coming from Waterford on the N25, after the town of Lemybrien, look for the resume speed sign. 5km later there is a right turn, travel 220m and you will see a sign for the house.

COAST TOWNHOUSE

Turlough McNamara & Jenny McNally
Upper Branch Road
Tramore, County Waterford
✆ **051-393646**
🖷 **051-393647**
🖰 **www.coast.ie**

The hippest, hottest couple, McNamara and McNally, run the hippest, hottest address in all of Ireland.

In a few years time, Turlough McNamara and Jenny McNally will preside over a small empire of the classiest food and hospitality addresses in Ireland. Already, in addition to the magnificent Coast, there is 33 The Mall in Waterford, and Shoebaloo, the grooviest footwear emporium in the country. And they have only started.

What's their secret? Well, apart from being very smart, what they do is to filter contemporary ideas that capture the zeitgeist of what people want, right now. That's why it's such fun to stay in Coast: you feel these four rooms, in their style and comfort, capture perfectly what you want the way you want it, right now. Like great designers such as Paddy Foyle and Ken Buggy, McNamara and McNally never, ever lapse into cliché. Everything they do, from design through to fantastic breakfasts, speaks of spontaneity and wit and culture. Their intelligence makes for exhilarating experiences, the empire has only begun.

- **OPEN:** All year
- **ROOMS:** Four rooms
- **PRICE:** €50-€80 per person sharing

- **NOTES:** 💳Visa, Mastercard, Laser.
Restaurant, Dinner served 6.30pm-10pm Tue-Sat, 1pm-3pm Sun, Dinner €40. Early bird €26.50, 6.30pm-7.30pm. No ઠ access.

- **DIRECTIONS:**
Take the R673 from Waterford city. Just up from the beach front road in Tramore, the entrance is on Upper Branch Road. Look for the signs.

GLASHA FARMHOUSE

Olive O'Gorman
Ballymacarbry
County Waterford
℡ 052-36108
🖰 www.glashafarmhouse.com

Olive O'Gorman's house is hugely popular with walkers, who cherish the monumental, amazing breakfasts, and look forward to tasty dinners.

It takes about two paragraphs to list all the wonderful things Olive O'Gorman presents and parades for breakfast every morning in Glasha, every manner of fruit, every manner of bread, every manner of egg dish, every manner of cereal, every manner of drink. "A delight – or a dilemma?", asked Arminta Wallace in *The Irish Times*.

Come on, Arminta! A delight, for sure: this is one of the very best breakfasts you can encounter in Ireland and, for the walkers in the Knockmealdown and Comeragh mountains, which many of the guests in Glasha are, it is the very thing to put a spring in your step as you set off to hike up a hill or two in the rain. And when you get back, soaked, exhausted, worn out, then there are comfortable rooms and a comfortable dinner to look forward to, friendly food that is just what you felt like eating. "Glasha is the kind of place I suspect you'd always be glad to come home to", writes Arminta Wallace. Too true.

● **OPEN:** all year, except Christmas
● **ROOMS:** Eight rooms, all en suite
● **PRICE:** B&B €100-€120 per room.
Single rate €50-€60

● **NOTES:** 💳Visa, Mastercard.
Dinner 7pm-8pm €25-€35, BYO. Children over 12 years welcome. Secure parking. ♿ access.
🖰 Email bookings.

● **DIRECTIONS:**
Well signposted, off the R671 between Clonmel and Dungarvan. 3km from Ballymacarbry.

GORTNADIHA

Eileen & Tom Harty
Ring
Dungarvan
County Waterford
✆ **058-46142**
🖰 **waterfordfarms.com/gortnadiha**

Eileen Harty's regular customers – all of them – have followed Mrs Harty to her new Ring address, right next door to the original Gortnadiha house.

How do you make a success of a hospitality business, specifically a country bed and breakfast? Well, you should set yourself a target of having, say, 60% of your business as repeat business, people who have been once, had the best time, and who then come back again because they want that best time one more time. If you can hit that target, then you are flying.

Eileen Harty hit that target some years back, within only a couple of years of opening her lovely Gortnadiha. And all those happy customers have followed Eileen to her new destination, next door to the original Gortnadiha.

Here, Mrs Harty has a smart house with amazing views over the bay, she has three smart, themed rooms, and whilst the destination has changed slightly, what won't be changing is the special gift this lady has for hospitality. That's why the 60% of the customers are regulars, folk for whom an escape to Ring always means: Gortnadiha.

● **OPEN:** 1 Feb-1 Dec
● **ROOMS:** Three rooms, all en suite
● **PRICE:** €30-€40 per person sharing, €10 single supplement

● **NOTES:** 💳Visa, Mastercard. No dinner. No ♿ access. Children welcome. Visa, Private parking.

● **DIRECTIONS:**
Follow the curve of Dungarvan Bay. Come off the N25 at the junction for Ring (3km west of Dungarvan). Signposted from here. Midway between Waterford and Cork. 2 hours from Rosslare.

10 SPLENDIDLY
REMOTE DESTINATIONS

1

ANNA'S HOUSE
COMBER, NORTHERN IRELAND

2

DOLPHIN BEACH
CLIFDEN, Co GALWAY

3

GREEN GATE
ARDARA, Co DONEGAL

4

HANORA'S COTTAGE
BALLYMACARBRY, Co WATERFORD

5

ISKEROON
CAHERDANIEL, Co KERRY

6

THE MILL
DUNFANAGHY, Co DONEGAL

7

MOSSIE'S
ADRIGOLE, Co CORK

8

RATHMULLAN HOUSE
RATHMULLAN, Co DONEGAL

9

RENVYLE
LETTERFRACK, Co GALWAY

10

STELLA MARIS
BALLYCASTLE, Co MAYO

HANORA'S COTTAGE

Mary Wall
Nire Valley, Ballymacarbry
County Waterford
✆ **052-36134**
🖷 **052-36540**
🖰 **www.hanorascottage.com**

The first time you encounter the
Hanora's breakfast is one of the great
travel experiences in Ireland, an
extraordinary cornucopia of foods.

One of our last visits to Hanora's Cottage coincided with
a blizzard, high up in the hills of the Nire Valley. Most
everyone who had booked to stay promptly cancelled, as
it was well nigh impossible to get there. And so, it hap-
pened that there were two guests that night, ourselves
and a hard-working medical rep. Did Hanora's take their
foot off the throttle? Were we given a bowl of cornflakes
for breakfast and a tea bag? Nope, not a bit of it. Eoin Wall
cooked us a solid dinner and, next morning, Mary Wall
prepared the gargantuan feast of deliciousness that is the
Hanora's breakfast as if there were 30 guests: the signature muesli (don't miss it!); poached plums; prunes; pome-
granates; apricots; local honey; Baylough cheese; fruit
scones; brown bread; yogurts; smoked salmon... and then
Mrs Wall asks, "And what would you like for a cooked
breakfast?" If that experience doesn't define hospitality,
then I'm afraid we just don't know what hospitality is.

● **OPEN:** All year, except Christmas
● **ROOMS:** 10 rooms
● **PRICE:** €75-€110 per person sharing.
Single room €85

● **NOTES:** Restaurant open 6.30pm-9pm.
♿ access. No children. Secure parking.
Special offers off season.
🖰 Email bookings.

● **DIRECTIONS:**
From Clonmel or Dungarvan, follow signs to
Ballymacarbry. The house is signposted from the bridge.

POWERSFIELD HOUSE

Eunice & Edmund Power
Ballinamuck West, Dungarvan
County Waterford
℗ **058-45594**
🖨 **058-45550**
🖰 **www.powersfield.com**

Cook, cookery teacher, catering company boss, hostess – it's all in a day's work for the multi-talented Eunice Power of Powersfield House.

Eunice Power is a fiercely self-critical person, and it is this very self-critical faculty that keeps Powersfield House on its toes. The house is a handsome modern building, just beside the Clonmel road, and it's a very comfortable, feminine place, decorated in deep, rich colours, a great chill-out environment that enjoys, as you would expect, brilliant housekeeping.

Mrs Power's cooking at dinner and breakfast shows another side of that self-critical faculty, for she is always exploring new ideas, cooking from new books, spinning off new ideas. That is one reason why her cookery classes are such a success – take one of these courses and you will have a rush of new ideas, and indeed you should take a course and stay over at Powersfield and make an event of a trip to west Waterford. Best of all, you can taste that creativity in the delicious food that Eunice takes such pleasure in preparing, food that makes PH special.

● **OPEN:** All year, except Christmas and New Year
● **ROOMS:** Six rooms, all en suite
● **PRICE:** €50-€60 per person sharing. Single room €60-€70

● **NOTES:** 🖃Amex, Visa, Mastercard, Laser.
Dinner for guests only, €27-€35.
Full wheelchair access. Children welcome.
🖰 On-line bookings.

● **DIRECTIONS:**
Follow Clonmel road from Dungarvan, the house is the second turn to the left, and the first house on the right.

RICHMOND HOUSE

Paul & Claire Deevy
Cappoquin
County Waterford
✆ **058-54278**
🖷 **058-54988**
🖱 **www.richmondhouse.net**

Richmond House is one of the very best places to eat and stay, with a charming, unpretentious naturalness.

"The food is really nice, the rooms are really nice with antlers and stuff, and it's not like a normal hotel."

It's no easy thing being the child of a pair of Bridgestone critics. When you get taken to Richmond House, Paul and Claire Deevy's elegant country house hotel just outside Cappoquin, you have to earn your supper. You have to have opinions! You have to say if you liked the room, the cooking, the staff. Poor kids!

Poor kids nothing. It is every kid's dream to be taken to a wonderful country house like Richmond, because, well, the food is really nice, the rooms are really nice with antlers and stuff and, above all, Richmond is not like a normal hotel. Richmond, in fact, is one of the most singular places to eat and stay in Ireland, and Mr and Mrs Deevy are amongst the best practitioners of the art of hospitality in Ireland. That's why the McKenna kids love it so much. And don't worry: adults love Richmond House too.

- **OPEN:** 20 Jan-20 Dec
- **ROOMS:** Nine rooms
- **PRICE:** from €75 per person sharing, Single supplement €20

- **NOTES:** 🖾 All major cards accepted.
Restaurant open for dinner only, Mon-Sun (closed on Sun in winter), €48.
Private parking. Children welcome, babysitting, toys.
🖱 On-line bookings.

- **DIRECTIONS:**
Just outside Cappoquin, the house is well signposted.

THE TANNERY TOWNHOUSE

Paul & Máire Flynn
10 Quay Street, Dungarvan
County Waterford
℡ 058-45420
🖷 058-45814
🖰 www.tannery.ie

The Tannery Townhouse was the newcomer that provided us with the best experience of the year in 2005.

Everyone always wants to know which destination provides the most memorable experience of the year for the Bridgestone Guides. This year, in the teeth of formidable competition, it was The Tannery Townhouse, Paul and Maire Flynn's super-cool, ultra-funky townhouse, an address so radical and so sophisticated that it raises the bar for all accommodation destinations in Ireland.

Every detail here has been thought through to give the guest the most cocooned experience possible. The rooms feel like cabins, but of the luxury liner style, not the below-decks variety. The style is pared down, again evoking the classic style of the cruise liner. Breakfast consists of fresh breads and pastries left on a hook outside your door last thing at night, whilst the fridge in the room has superb fruits, yogurts, juices, and you brew you own tea and coffee. The experience, then, is one of blissful abandonment, in an environment of sublime luxury.

- **OPEN:** All year, except Christmas
- **ROOMS:** Seven rooms, all en suite
- **PRICE:** from €50 per person sharing, Single €70

- **NOTES:** 🖮All major cards accepted. The Tannery Restaurant is open for lunch and dinner, dinner €45-€50. Two private parking spaces (first come first serve, otherwise street parking). 🖰 Email bookings.

- **DIRECTIONS:**
20m from The Tannery Restaurant, at the end of Main Street, which is just down from the main square, beside the Old Market House building.

TEMPLE COUNTRY HOUSE & HEALTH SPA

Declan & Bernadette Fagan
Horseleap, Moate, Co Westmeath
✆ **0506-35118**
🖷 **0506-35008**
🖱 **www.templespa.ie**

With the building work of the last year almost complete, Declan and Bernadette Fagan's Temple Spa is all set to emerge as a key destination.

Last year we reported how Declan and Bernadette Fagan, faced with the gargantuan task of enlarging their Temple Spa into a new complex with 23 rooms, seemed as calm as all get out at the daunting prospect facing them. This is a tribute to their calm nature, the very natures that make the Spa such a special place for so many people.

But, there is even more to their calmness, for whilst all the hullabaloo has been going on around them all during 2005, they have continued to run Temple as both guest house and spa, looking after their customers, cooking delicious food – roasted red pepper and carrot soup; rack of lamb with rosemary jus, steamed potatoes, peas with fresh mint and ratatouille; raspberry and honey creme fraiche pots – as their new building has slowly begun to emerge. In short, at Temple Declan and Bernadette practice what they preach: the sense of calmness and contemplation is real, and Temple is a true spa.

● **OPEN:** All year, except Christmas
● **ROOMS:** Eight rooms, all en suite
● **PRICE:** All inclusive rates:24 hour escape €235 p.p.s. for 24hrs midweek, Single €255.Spa Weekends from €435 p.p.s. Fri-Sun, €475 single.

● **NOTES:** 📼Visa, Mastercard, Access, Amex. Dinner, 8pm. Inclusive rates only. No wheelchair access. Children over 16 years. 🖱 On-line bookings.

● **DIRECTIONS:**
1km off the N6 Dublin-Galway road, and clearly signposted just after Horseleap, heading westwards.

WINEPORT LODGE

Jane English & Ray Byrne
Glassan, Athlone
County Westmeath
℗ 090-643 9010
🖷 090-648 5471
www.wineport.ie

Wineport Lodge has entered the national psyche as one of the greatest escapes for stressed-out city dwellers.

Ray Byrne and Jane English are amongst the great pioneers of Irish food and hospitality, people who first of all created a destination restaurant in Wineport, in an area and a place that was previously overlooked, and who have worked long and hard thereafter to promote Westmeath as a destination.

In that regard, of course, their courage in building on their hotel rooms has been the most significant thing they have achieved and, typically, they did it in an organic way, building first one section, then stepping up to 20 rooms, thereby showing the same steady sensible method of progression that has marked their work. The couple have always managed to make everything they do seem logical, simply because they have always done things so well, not least the utterly classic design and fit-out of the rooms, which makes them an extra-special retreat. The lake, the rooms, the restaurant, the wines combine to make magic.

- **OPEN:** All year
- **ROOMS:** 21 rooms
- **PRICE:** B&B €165-€395 per double room. Weekend breaks also.

- **NOTES:** 📷All major cards accepted. Restaurant serves dinner, à la carte menu approx €55. ♿ access. 🖰 On-line bookings.

- **DIRECTIONS:**
At Athlone, take the Longford exit off Dublin/Galway rd, fork left at the Dog & Duck, Lodge is 1.5km further on on the left.

BALLINKEELE HOUSE

John & Margaret Maher
Enniscorthy
County Wexford
✆ 053-38105
🖷 053-38468
🖰 www.ballinkeele.com

John and Margaret Maher's
lovely country house has
sky-high standards, making
for someplace special.

"Stayed a night at Ballinkeele House in Ballymurn, near
Enniscorthy, Co. Wexford. It's a lovely old place in impecca-
ble condition, with 350 acres, and a beautiful garden. John
Maher, who looks like an old movie star, is totally low-key
and charming - the perfect host. John's wife, Margaret does
the cooking, and the food is delicious: we had venison shot
by a friend of the owners, delicious crème brûlée and
bananas Foster for dessert; and a lovely breakfast, too.
Everything at a super high standard. Would definitely recom-
mend for top 100 places to stay."
Well, that is about as unequivocal as unequivocal can get
from a Bridgestone editor, wouldn't you say? Movie star
good looks. Super high standards. Beautiful house and gardens. Food from the region cooked perfectly at both dinner
and breakfast. And when did you last have bananas Foster?
John and Margaret really make a special effort at Ballinkeele,
and it makes for a great country house experience.

- **OPEN:** Open Feb-end of the Opera Festival
- **ROOMS:** 5 double rooms, all en suite
- **PRICE:** €70-€85 per person sharing,
Single suppl. €20

- **NOTES:** 🖃All major cards accepted. Dinner €40,
please book by 11.30am. Children welcome, but no
under 12s allowed in dining room at dinner.
🖰 On-line bookings taken.

- **DIRECTIONS:**
From Wexford, take the N11, and the house is signposted on your right.

KELLY'S RESORT HOTEL

Bill Kelly
Rosslare
County Wexford
℡ **053-32114**
🖷 **053-32222**
🖰 **www.kellys.ie**

The Kelly family regard hospitality as an act of public service, which is what makes Kelly's so unique.

Why does Kelly's Resort Hotel succeed so well at the very many things it does? Simple. Bill Kelly and his team run their hotel as a testament to the idea of hospitality as a form of public service. Of course they have to make a profit, but unlike so many modern places to eat and stay, making a profit is not the be-all and end-all of Kelly's. Much more important to them is the idea of hospitality as an expression of culture, and in this regard the work of the Kelly family can be seen more as a vocation than a profession – the vocation of hospitality, and hospitality as a public service, is what they offer.

This offer comes with fabulous cooking, the most gorgeous design, a fantastic spa, and an overall atmosphere that is utterly unlike any other place to stay in Ireland. Everything about Kelly's is so confident, so disciplined and principled, that it really does transform the way you look at life. In that sense, the entire hotel is a spa, for the soul.

- ● **OPEN:** Late Feb-early Dec
- ● **ROOMS:** 116 rooms, all en suite
- ● **PRICE:** Spring/autumn: weekend rate €300pp + 10% service charge; 5-day midweek from €580pp + 10% service charge. Summer: 7-day rate from €895pp + 10%

- ● **NOTES:** 🖾All major cards accepted. All rates include full board. La Marine restaurant also comes recommended. ♿ access. Every facility for babies and children.

- ● **DIRECTIONS:**
Clearly signposted in Rosslare and from the main Wexford-Rosslare Harbour road.

McMENAMIN'S TOWNHOUSE

Seamus & Kay McMenamin
3 Auburn Terrace
Redmond Road, Wexford
County Wexford
✆ 053-46442
🖰 www.wexford-bedandbreakfast.com

north
east
west
south

Seamus and Kay McMenamin's elegant Wexford townhouse epitomises hospitality, and thrives on great attention paid to every single detail.

Here is the sort of letter that, if you run a townhouse or an hotel or a B&B or whatever, that you would dream about someone writing to the Bridgestone Guides:
"Seamus and Kay epitomise the spirit of hospitality that permeates Ireland. The attention to detail is outstanding, in both the accommodation and the breakfasts."
Well, you can shoot the critic when it's the customers giving you feedback like that. But what is interesting about this letter is the significance it attaches to "the attention to detail", for that is the secret of this comfortable townhouse, which is literally a stone's throw from the centre of Wexford town. It is all very well being the epitomisation of hospitality, but if you don't remember that God – or the Devil, take your pick – is in the detail, then you are toast. Seamus and Kay McMenamin never forget the detail, and that is what keeps them at the top of their game. Oh, and don't, don't miss the Donegal pancakes.

- **OPEN:** All year, except Christmas
- **ROOMS:** Seven rooms, all en suite
- **PRICE:** €45 per person sharing. Single €50

- **NOTES:** 💳Visa, Mastercard. No dinner.
No wheelchair access.
Locked parking. Children welcome, high chair, cot, babysitting. 🖰 On-line bookings.

- **DIRECTIONS:**
In the centre of Wexford, directly opposite the bus and railway stations. Beside the large Dunnes Stores supermarket.

SALVILLE HOUSE

Jane & Gordon Parker
Salville, Enniscorthy
County Wexford
✆ **054-35252**
📠 **054-35252**
🖱 **www.salvillehouse.com**

Any producer who wants
to make a series on Irish
country cooking has to
start with Gordon Parker.

All of the houses in the Bridgestone 100 win praise from
the people who visit them during the year, but what is
most consistent about the praise won by Jane and
Gordon Parker's Salville House – "It's a beautiful, relaxing
place" – is the praise won for Gordon Parker's cooking –
"The best part was the food which was really lovely".
Mr Parker is amongst the very best country house cooks,
but his style owes more to the professional kitchen than
to the accomplished amateur. Truth be told, this guy could
hack it in any professional set up, such is the individuality
and signature of his food, and he works lovely themes
with fish dishes in particular, serving john dory one day
with a gazpacho couscous, and another day varying it by
serving roasted Mediterranean vegetables with the fish.
Bring your very best bottles to pay tribute to this food,
and then enjoy the peace and comfort of the houses; 3
colourful rooms, or the pretty 2-roomed apartment.

● **OPEN:** All year, except Christmas
● **ROOMS:** Five rooms. One two-bedroom self-con-
tained apartment available for B&B or self catering
● **PRICE:** €45-€50 per person sharing

● **NOTES:** No credit cards.
Dinner, 8pm, €35. Book 24 hours in advance.
No ♿ access. Secure parking. 🖱 Email bookings.

● **DIRECTIONS:**
Leaving Enniscorthy on the N11 to Wexford, take the
first left after the hospital, go up the hill to a T-junction
then turn left and proceed for 500m

BALLYKNOCKEN HOUSE

Catherine Fulvio
Glenealy, Ashford
County Wicklow
✆ **0404-44627**
🖷 **0404-44696**
www.ballyknocken.com

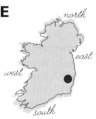

Cook, hostess and cookery teacher, Catherine Fulvio pulls off these disparate roles with easy aplomb.

"Went to Ballyknocken House for a night... and were blown away by Catherine and her hospitality."
We get loads of stuff like this about Catherine Fulvio's house, her hospitality, and her cooking – "a fabulous meal which we are still raving about" – and, to be honest, it doesn't come as a surprise. Mrs Fulvio is one of the most focused and most gifted of hospitality practitioners. We knew her first when she worked in marketing for hotels, and she was truly exceptional in that role also.
But, as cook and hostess and cookery teacher in Ballyknocken House, Mrs Fulvio has truly blossomed. She combines the drive of Darina Allen with the culinary subtlety of Maura Foley, and you can't say better than that. Like Mrs Foley, her cooking is a very personal take on contemporary country cooking, rich in flavour, deeply satisfying, and hugely generous, and it is that generosity that is her secret. It's a real treat to stay here, no mistake.

● **OPEN:** Feb-Nov
● **ROOMS:** Seven rooms
● **PRICE:** From €55-€62 per person sharing. Single supplement €28

● **NOTES:** 💳Visa, Mastercard. Dinner, Mon-Sat, €38. No ♿ access. Children welcome. Cookery school. ⌂ On-line bookings. Short break rates online.

● **DIRECTIONS:**
From Dublin, head south to Ashford (on N11), then turn right after Chester Beatty pub. Continue for 5km and the house is on the right.

THE BROOK LODGE INN

Evan, Eoin & Bernard Doyle
Macreddin Village, Aughrim
County Wicklow
℡ 0402-36444
℡ 0402-36580
🖱 www.brooklodge.com

The Brook Lodge Inn is so famous it has become the object of satire. Come on down, Ross O'C-K...

Evan Doyle's country hotel is so famous that it is already, only five years after opening, the subject of satire. When Sorcha, the wife of the legendary Ross O'Carroll Kelly, uber-oaf creation of *The Sunday Tribune's* Paul Howard, takes a few days off for some "pampering, roysh, some me time as she calls it", then where does she go? That's right: "Brook Lodge in Wicklow". As one would expect with Ross O'C K, he can't even get the name correct.

But, the Brook Lodge Inn is indeed where Dubliners go for that "me time", to enjoy superb cooking, a glorious green-field environment, a chance to escape from the maddening city that is Dublin. The success of the Brook Lodge Inn is such that it tends to be taken for granted, but what Evan Doyle and his crew have achieved in Macreddin is one of the great feats of Irish hospitality. The Brook Lodge Inn succeeds because it is a centre of culture, a place where Irish hospitality is at its very best.

● **OPEN:** All year, including Christmas
● **ROOMS:** 55 rooms and suites
● **PRICE:** €105-€120 per person sharing, single supplements apply. Check web for rates for B&B and Dinner.

● **NOTES:** 🖃All major cards accepted. Restaurant, pubs, market and bakery, dinner €55. Secure car parking. Reservations essential. No ♿ access. Children welcome. 🖱 On-line bookings.

● **DIRECTIONS:**
N11 to Rathnew. Right at r'about, to Glenealy, on to Rathdrum. 1.5km outside Rathdrum, right towards Aughrim.

ANNA'S HOUSE

Anna Johnson
Tullynagee, 35 Lisbarnett Rd
Comber, County Down
✆ **028-9754 1566**
🖷 **028-9754 1566**
🖰 **www.annashouse.com**

Anna and Ken's house is one of the ultimate cult addresses, with fans from all over the world.

Anna and Ken Johnson's house is the ultimate cult destination in Northern Ireland. A gorgeous house, a gorgeous garden, gorgeous cooking, Anna's is the sort of house that manages to evoke the most elemental feelings about hospitality, food and our place in the world.

Anna's is 14 miles from Belfast, but feels a zillion miles from the real world. Step in here and you step into a dream, or at least into some imagined world from your childhood, a space where you are woken by the smells of morning baking, a space where you can lose yourself in an afternoon in the garden, where you can chat away to people you have just met and yet feel you have known them all your life. Does that sound like hyperbole? Well check this script from a pair of German visitors: "This is the ideal B&B... great cooking, comfy rooms and superb hospitality. Anna and Ken you're great.. it felt like coming home." Feels like coming home.

● **OPEN:** All year, except Christmas
● **ROOMS:** Three rooms
● **PRICE:** £40-£45 per single room, £70 double room

● **NOTES:** Dinner by request. Secure car parking. No ♿ access. Babies welcome, not suitable for children. 🖰 On-line bookings.

● **DIRECTIONS:**
In Lisbane pass the petrol station, turn right into Lisbarnett Road. After 1km & after a right-hand bend follow a private concrete lane leading up the hill.

BALLYMOTE HOUSE

Nicola & James Manningham-Buller
Killough Road
Downpatrick
County Down
℡ **028-4461 5500**
⌂ **www.ballymotehouse.com**

Resplendent, elegantly
faded charm and great
cooking from Nicola are
the Ballymote signatures.

If you're a food-lover looking for somewhere to stay in St
Patrick's country, then there's nowhere nicer than
Ballymote, a pretty Georgian B&B and well worn family
home, stuffed full of fine hand-me-down antiques, faded
silk curtains and pure-bred dogs.

Blissful beds, huge bathtubs, log and hand-cut-turf fires
await you, and Nicola, an enthusiastic, well practiced
cook, gives ingredients - from local butchers, the family
estate, and the boats at Ardglass - a sophisticated cordon
bleu treatment. You need to allow plenty of advance
warning if there's a large party, or if you'd like to experience the aristocratic charm of the dining room. However,
even at short notice, Nicola will churn out delicious sup-
pers – such as the legendary stone of langoustines and
bottle of Chablis - while chattering away about horsey
pursuits and all the activities you can pursue in this beautiful holy well and stone circle-blessed countryside.

● **OPEN:** All year, except Christmas
● **ROOMS:** Three rooms
● **PRICE:** B&B £35 per person.

● **NOTES:** ▭Visa, Mastercard. ⌂ Email bookings. Pets
facilitated, but not in the house. Horses can be stabled
by arrangement. Preferably no children under 5 yrs.
Secure parking. No ♿ access. Internet access available to
guests.

● **DIRECTIONS:**
In Downpatrick, take the B176 to Killough and they are
1.5km on the left-hand side.

10 PLACES
KIDS WILL LOVE

1
BALLYNAHINCH CASTLE
RECESS, Co GALWAY

2
GHAN HOUSE
CARLINGFORD, Co LOUTH

3
GROVE HOUSE
SCHULL, Co CORK

4
INN AT CASTLEDAWSON
CASTLEDAWSON, NORTHERN IRELAND

5
KELLY'S RESORT HOTEL
ROSSLARE, Co WEXFORD

6
THE KILLARNEY PARK HOTEL
KILLARNEY, Co KERRY

7
THE MILL
DUNFANAGHY, Co DONEGAL

8
OTTO'S CREATIVE CATERING
BUTLERSTOWN, Co CORK

9
POWERSFIELD HOUSE
DUNGARVAN, Co WATERFORD

10
RATHMULLAN HOUSE
RATHMULLAN Co DONEGAL

THE CARRIAGE HOUSE

Maureen Griffith
71 Main Street, Dundrum
County Down
℡ **028-4375 1635**
🖱 **www.carriagehousedundrum.com**

Maureen Griffith's charming house is composed like an artist's palette: colourful, creative, spirited and fine, just perfect for exploring the region.

A handsome and unannounced house right next door to The Buck's Head Inn in Dundrum, The Carriage House is bright and uncluttered, and Maureen Griffith's interiors sympathetically juxtapose delicate antiques with authentic retro and modern furnishings, and display a personal and eclectic selection of art. Her three bedrooms are homely and indulgent, with tasteful, treat-filled trays, powerful showers, fresh flowers, finely perfumed soaps, and plump beds piled high with soft pillows in fine cotton. Breakfasts are also a delight, as you would expect from someone with a true professional's touch and experience, with just-made fruit salads, star-anise spiced plums, herby sausages, and local or homemade breads. Her sun-exposed garden, with fabulous horse sculpture, has lovely views over Dundrum Bay and is a playground for pet labradors, hedgehogs, and grandchildren in this most relaxing home from home. You won't want to leave.

● **OPEN:** All year
● **ROOMS:** Three rooms, all en suite
● **PRICE:** £60 double room, Single room £40

● **NOTES:** 💳 Visa, Mastercard.
No dinner, but excellent restaurant, The Buck's Head, just next door. Children welcome.
5 minutes from Royal County Down Golf Club,
No ♿ access. 🖱 Email bookings.

● **DIRECTIONS:**
Dundrum is on the main Belfast to Newcastle Road (A24), and The Carriage House is in the centre of town.

FERNDALE

Peter Mills
Irvinestown Road, Enniskillen
County Fermanagh
℡ **028-6632 8374**
🖰 **www.ferndalecountry-**
houseandrestaurant.com

Peter Mills has some work
to do on the style of
Ferndale to get it to match
the fiery élan of his cooking.

It's a sign of the focus on care and anticipation of the customer's needs that the door at Ferndale will most likely
be opened for you even before you have got to the
threshold of this restaurant with rooms, just on the outskirts of Enniskillen. Peter Mills has serious ambitions to
get realised over the next few years, and he has already
made a promising start in terms of his cooking.
In terms of design, he has a lot of work ahead of him,
though the house has nice high ceilings, open fires, heavy
panel doors, and lots of interesting paintings by local
artists. But there is an homogenisation that needs to be
overcome, so that the style has the élan of the cooking.
And that cooking is why most folk will choose to come
to Ferndale, and to have an overnight, for this kitchen has
some serious skill, and when service is tightened up, all
should go swimmingly. Breakfasts, meantime, are excellent, in particular an organic breakfast that is only ace.

● **OPEN:** All year
● **ROOMS:** Six rooms
● **PRICE:** £27-£37.50 per person sharing, £10 single
supplement.

● **NOTES:** ▨Mastercard, Visa. Restaurant open dinner
& Sun lunch. No ♿ access. Secure parking.
🖰 Email booking.

● **DIRECTIONS:**
Coming from Enniskillen, cross the Cherrymount
roundabout, then travel 1km on the
Irvinstown road. Ferndale is on your right.

THE INN AT CASTLEDAWSON

Simon Toye & Kathy Tully
47 Main Street
Castledawson, County Londonderry
℃ **048-7946 9777**
🖰 **www.theinnatcastledawson.co.uk**

north
east
west
south

Simon and Kathy's newcom-
er is a dynamic address with
infinite potential to be a
major player 'oop North.

Simon Toye and Kathy Tully have serious backgrounds in
the restaurant business, with spells working for Nick
Price and Paul Rankin in Belfast before they moved to
Castledawson and opened up shop together. Between the
two of them, they have just the right energy to create a
destination address, here in the pretty Inn.

Ms Tully is dynamic, helpful and knowledgeable, and runs
front-of-house with assured ease. Mr Toye, meanwhile,
cooks with a relaxed confidence: smoked Lough Neagh
eel with organic leaves and horseradish is a smashing
dish; rolled belly of pork is sweet and delicious; perfect
roast vegetables; burnt orange crème caramel is right on
the money. Service and food is tip-top. The bedrooms are
modern and provide a perfect excuse to make a night of
it away from the city and the kids, something many cou-
ples will soon discover. The Inn has enormous potential:
we look forward to its progress.

- ● **OPEN:** All year
- ● **ROOMS:** 12 rooms
- ● **PRICE:** £35-£40 for double room, £50 single room

- ● **NOTES:** 📧 Mastercard, Visa, Switch, Maestro.
Restaurant open lunch & dinner.
♿ access.
Secure parking for 12 cars.
Children welcome, children's menu. Under 15s £10.
🖰 Email enquiries.

- ● **DIRECTIONS:**
On the main street, just down from the church.

MARLAGH LODGE

Robert & Rachel Thompson
71 Moorfields Road
Ballymena
County Antrim
℡ **028-2563 1505**
🖱 **www.marlaghlodge.com**

Robert and Rachel's restoration of Marlagh is complete, and showcases their skills as designers.

All is cool, calm and comfortable at Marlagh Lodge - after a mammoth two-year restoration project on this gorgeous, sumptuous Victorian listed building – and Robert and Rachel are onto their next 'harebrained' scheme, they say, running gourmet evenings with wine merchant James Nicholson. Well actually we think it's a jolly sensible idea, because as well as consummate musicians, interior designers, and hosts, they're accomplished cooks. A sweet and salty salad of roasted pears, Cashel blue and toasted walnuts, might be followed by fillet of beef with butter-roasted shallots or a roasted red pepper, goat's cheese and poppy seed tartlet. Refreshing summer desserts include a fresh raspberry and blueberry jelly with mint cream. You can just book for dinner party style eating, but staying in Marlagh Lodge's exquisitely detailed rooms, and Rachel's whiskey-laced porridge, are indulgences you won't easily forget.

- **OPEN:** Open all year
- **ROOMS:** Three rooms, all en suite
- **PRICE:** B&B £70 per room, £35 single

- **NOTES:**
Mastercard, Visa, Switch, Maestro.
Dinner, 8pm (book by noon), £10.50
No & access.
Children welcome. 🖱 Email bookings.

- **DIRECTIONS:**
From the A36 to Larne, turn onto Rankinstown Road, and the driveway is immediately on your left.

PAUL ARTHURS

Paul Arthurs
66 Main Street
Kircubbin
County Down
© **028-4273 8192**
www.paul/arthurs.com

The Paul Arthurs machine is gearing up to be one of the key destination addresses in all of Northern Ireland.

Paul Arthurs has introduced the dynamic concept of the Restaurant with Rooms to Northern Ireland, adding on seven bedrooms to his restaurant – and chip shop – in the centre of Kircubbin. It's a smart move: Mr Arthurs food is worth travelling for, and being able to make a night of it down the peninsula with comfortable, inexpensive rooms is good news.

The rooms have oodles of character, thanks to the use of exposed brick and moody paintings, and the bathrooms are full-scale wet rooms with dark slate floors and powerful showers. The doors are at present a little bit creaky and hard to manage, and consequently create quite a lot of noise, but the linens are good, the towels are good – though toiletries should be provided. And breakfast, whilst somewhat predictable, is well-executed in the bright dining room. Everything reveals the care and attention to detail of a good crew, and PA shouldn't be missed.

● **OPEN:** Open all year, except Jan
● **ROOMS:** Seven rooms, all en suite
● **PRICE:** £70 per double room, sharing. Single room £50. £10 supplement for children sharing room.

● **NOTES:**
Visa, Mastercard.
Dinner in Paul Arthurs' restaurant, £28.
Stair lift for disabled. Email bookings.

● **DIRECTIONS:**
Right in the middle of main street in the village, on the left-hand side as you drive towards Portaferry.

INDEX

Keep in touch with what's happening in Irish food

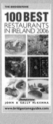

see our complete catalogue at
www.bridgestoneguides.com

www.bridgestoneguides.com publishes regular updates to entries listed in the Bridgestone Guides, as well as links to hundreds of good web addresses in Irish Food. There is also an on-line service for buying books.

Sign up for our website newsletter Megabytes, and we'll be sure to keep you posted.